A Retreat With Black Elk

Other titles in the
A Retreat With... *Series:*

A Retreat With Black Elk

Living in the Sacred Hoop

Marie Therese Archambault, O.S.F.

ST. ANTHONY MESSENGER PRESS

Cincinnati, Ohio

Scripture citations are taken from the *New Revised Standard Version Bible*, copyright ©1989 by the Division of Christian Education of the National Council of Churches of Christ in the U.S.A. and used by permission.

The excerpts from *Lone Dog's Winter Count*, by Diane Glancy, copyright ©1991, by West End Press; *Voices of Earth and Sky: The Vision Life of the Native Americans*, by Vinson Brown, copyright ©1976, by Naturegraph Publishers, Inc.; *The Sixth Grandfather: Black Elk's Teachings Given to John G. Neihardt*, ed. Raymond J. DeMallie, copyright ©1985, by University of Nebraska Press; *Red Cloud's Folk: A History of the Oglala Sioux Indians*, by George E. Hyde, copyright ©1979, by the University of Oklahoma Press; *Black Elk and Flaming Rainbow: Personal Memories of the Lakota Holy Man and John Neihardt*, by Hilda Neihardt, copyright ©1995, by the University of Nebraska Press; *Black Elk: Holy Man of the Oglala*, by Michael F. Steltenkamp, copyright © 1993, by the University of Oklahoma Press; *The Sioux: Life and Customs of a Warrior Society, Civilization of the American Indian Series, Vol. 72*, by Royal B. Hassrick, copyright ©1964 by the University of Oklahoma Press; *Civilization of the American Indian Series, Vol. 36*, by the University of Oklahoma Press, copyright ©1953, by the University of Oklahoma Press; *Selected Poetry of Jessica Powers*, ed. Siegfried and Morneau, copyright ©1989, by Sheed & Ward, are used by permission of the publishers.

Cover and book design by Mary Alfieri
Electronic format and pagination by Sandra Digman

ISBN 0-86716-271-6

Copyright ©1998, Marie Therese Archambault

All rights reserved.

Published by St. Anthony Messenger Press
Printed in the U.S.A.

Contents

Introducing A Retreat With...

Twenty years ago I made a weekend retreat at a Franciscan house on the coast of New Hampshire. The retreat director's opening talk was as lively as a long-range weather forecast. He told us how completely God loves each one of us—without benefit of lively anecdotes or fresh insights.

As the friar rambled on, my inner critic kept up a sotto voce commentary: "I've heard all this before." "Wish he'd say something new that I could chew on." "That poor man really doesn't have much to say." Ever hungry for manna yet untasted, I devalued any experience of hearing the same old thing.

After a good night's sleep, I awoke feeling as peaceful as a traveler who has at last arrived safely home. I walked across the room toward the closet. On the way I passed the sink with its small framed mirror on the wall above. Something caught my eye like an unexpected presence. I turned, saw the reflection in the mirror and said aloud, "No wonder he loves me!"

This involuntary affirmation stunned me. What or whom had I seen in the mirror? When I looked again, it was "just me," an ordinary person with a lower-than-average reservoir of self-esteem. But I knew that in the initial vision I had seen God-in-me breaking through like a sudden sunrise.

At that moment I knew what it meant to be made in the divine image. I understood right down to my size eleven feet what it meant to be loved exactly as I was. Only later did I connect this revelation with one granted to the Trappist monk-writer Thomas Merton. As he reports in *Conjectures of a Guilty Bystander*, while standing all unsuspecting on a street corner one day, he was overwhelmed by the "joy of being...a member of a race in which God Himself became incarnate.... There is no way of telling people that they are all walking around shining like the sun."

As an absentminded homemaker may leave a wedding ring on the kitchen windowsill, so I have often mislaid this precious conviction. But I have never forgotten that particular retreat. It persuaded me that the Spirit rushes in where it will. Not even a boring director or a judgmental retreatant can withstand the "violent wind" that "fills the entire house" where we dwell in expectation (see Acts 2:2).

So why deny ourselves any opportunity to come aside awhile and rest on holy ground? Why not withdraw from the daily web that keeps us muddled and wound? Wordsworth's complaint is ours as well: "The world is too much with us." There is no flu shot to protect us from infection by the skepticism of the media, the greed of commerce, the alienating influence of technology. We need retreats as the deer needs the running stream.

An Invitation

This book and its companions in the *A Retreat With...* series from St. Anthony Messenger Press are designed to meet that need. They are an invitation to choose as director some of the most powerful, appealing and wise mentors our faith tradition has to offer.

Our directors come from many countries, historical

eras and schools of spirituality. At times they are teamed to sing in close harmony (for example, Francis de Sales, Jane de Chantal and Aelred of Rievaulx on spiritual friendship). Others are paired to kindle an illuminating fire from the friction of their differing views (such as Augustine of Hippo and Mary Magdalene on human sexuality). All have been chosen because, in their humanness and their holiness, they can help us grow in self-knowledge, discernment of God's will and maturity in the Spirit.

Inviting us into relationship with these saints and holy ones are inspired authors from today's world, women and men whose creative gifts open our windows to the Spirit's flow. As a motto for the authors of our series, we have borrowed the advice of Dom Frederick Dunne to the young Thomas Merton. Upon joining the Trappist monks, Merton wanted to sacrifice his writing activities lest they interfere with his contemplative vocation. Dom Frederick wisely advised, "Keep on writing books that make people love the spiritual life."

That is our motto. Our purpose is to foster (or strengthen) friendships between readers and retreat directors—friendships that feed the soul with wisdom, past and present. Like the scribe "trained for the kingdom of heaven," each author brings forth from his or her storeroom "what is new and what is old" (Matthew 13:52).

The Format

The pattern for each *A Retreat With...* remains the same; readers of one will be in familiar territory when they move on to the next. Each book is organized as a seven-session retreat that readers may adapt to their own schedules or to the needs of a group.

Day One begins with an anecdotal introduction called "Getting to Know Our Directors." Readers are given a telling glimpse of the guides with whom they will be sharing the retreat experience. A second section, "Placing Our Directors in Context," will enable retreatants to see the guides in their own historical, geographical, cultural and spiritual settings.

Having made the human link between seeker and guide, the authors go on to "Introducing Our Retreat Theme." This section clarifies how the guide(s) are especially suited to explore the theme and how the retreatant's spirituality can be nourished by it.

After an original "Opening Prayer" to breathe life into the day's reflection, the author, speaking with and through the mentor(s), will begin to spin out the theme. While focusing on the guide(s)' own words and experience, the author may also draw on Scripture, tradition, literature, art, music, psychology or contemporary events to illuminate the path.

Each day's session is followed by reflection questions designed to challenge, affirm and guide the reader in integrating the theme into daily life. A "Closing Prayer" brings the session full circle and provides a spark of inspiration for the reader to harbor until the next session.

Days Two through Six begin with "Coming Together in the Spirit" and follow a format similar to Day One. Day Seven weaves the entire retreat together, encourages a continuation of the mentoring relationship and concludes with "Deepening Your Acquaintance," an envoi to live the theme by God's grace, the director(s)' guidance and the retreatant's discernment. A closing section of Resources serves as a larder from which readers may draw enriching books, videos, cassettes and films.

We hope readers will experience at least one of those

memorable "No wonder God loves me!" moments. And we hope that they will have "talked back" to the mentors, as good friends are wont to do.

A case in point: There was once a famous preacher who always drew a capacity crowd to the cathedral. Whenever he spoke, an eccentric old woman sat in the front pew directly beneath the pulpit. She took every opportunity to mumble complaints and contradictions—just loud enough for the preacher to catch the drift that he was not as wonderful as he was reputed to be. Others seated down front glowered at the woman and tried to shush her. But she went right on needling the preacher to her heart's content.

When the old woman died, the congregation was astounded at the depth and sincerity of the preacher's grief. Asked why he was so bereft, he responded, "Now who will help me to grow?"

All of our mentors in *A Retreat With...* are worthy guides. Yet none would seek retreatants who simply said, "Where you lead, I will follow. You're the expert." In truth, our directors provide only half the retreat's content. Readers themselves will generate the other half.

As general editor for the retreat series, I pray that readers will, by their questions, comments, doubts and decision-making, fertilize the seeds our mentors have planted.

And may the Spirit of God rush in to give the growth.

Gloria Hutchinson
Series Editor
Conversion of Saint Paul, 1995

Getting to Know Our Director

Black Elk has been called a spiritual genius by many, credited with the reawakening and recovery of the pan-Native American ritual and spiritual tradition in the United States. His books, *Black Elk Speaks*, *When the Tree Flowered* and *The Sacred Pipe*, all published by 1952, sparked a movement for the recovery of Native American spiritual customs. *Black Elk Speaks* has been translated into several languages, demonstrating that his ideas have an international audience. Many Native American people, not only the Lakota, consider it the Indian "Bible." Black Elk's life reflected his conviction that his people could live again spiritually in two ways: through the Catholic tradition he embraced and through the ancient Lakota traditions. Perhaps the fact that his works speak to many people, both Indian and non-Indian, indicates a spiritual hunger for his holistic vision. The books which he has left us fill an emptiness within—the earmark of spiritual genius.

As evidence of the continuing interest in Black Elk's thought, it has only been ten years since anthropologist Raymond DeMallie published *The Sixth Grandfather*, an English translation of the original stenographic notes of Enid Neihardt (wife of Black Elk's first editor). Also, in 1993, anthropologist and Jesuit Michael Steltenkamp's book, *Black Elk: Holy Man of the Oglala*, was published. In it, Black Elk's only daughter, Lucy Looks Twice, testifies that her father was a well-known Catholic catechist and missionary during the greater part of his life. He lived his last forty-six years as a staunch Catholic and firm teacher of its faith among the Oglala and several Upper Plains tribes.

Even after his long tenure as a catechist, Black Elk referred to life blooming forth from the metaphorical sacred tree at the center of the people, rather than only from the salvation of the Church. We must, however, also look carefully at the witness of his life which fully supports his Catholicity. Perhaps he was unable to totally abandon the truth and universality of either his Lakota way or his Catholic convictions, even though their expressions of this truth at times seemed contradictory. Or perhaps his philosophy was a synthesis of both that transcended these contradictions. This we will never know for sure.

Our retreat with Black Elk draws on firsthand documents of his heritage and life (See Deepening Your Acquaintance, pages 103-104). This book is an attempt to listen to his prayer and accompany him from there. We Native American Christians, especially, seek and pray for wisdom to allow these ancient traditions to enlighten and heal us. But because this book presents Black Elk's spiritual teaching within the Christian context of a retreat, it allows many people to appreciate his unique, holistic vision.

Out of respect for the Lakota religion of the pipe, I will not advocate the use of the pipe for this retreat. Black Elk prayed with the pipe even in his last years, and the ceremonies and ritual in this book all surround the pipe as their center in sacred Lakota tradition. However, its use for praying in the directions has been omitted in this retreat because of its centrality and critical meaning for many contemporary tribal people. I wanted to avoid confusion between the Lakota and Catholic traditions and, in Black Elk's spirit, to honor the integrity of both. Our retreat will allow each to stand in its own right as much as possible.

Lakota Pronunciation Key

For words used in this book

heyoka [ha **yo** ka] — sacred clown, empowered by the West

hokshila [hohk **shee** lah] — boy

Iapi Oaye [ee **yah** pee oh yay] — Word Carrier

Kahnigapi [kagh **nee** gah pi] — "they chose him"

okolakiciyapi [oh kolah **kee** ci yah pi] — Lakota societies

Skan [skhanh] — sky

tioshpaye [tee **osh** pay yay] — family grouping

Unci Maka [un **chi** mah kah] — grandmother earth

ushica [**un** shi kah] — pitiful, in need of mercy

ushimala [un **shi** mah lah] — Please, have mercy on me!

ushikiciyapi [unshi **kee** chee yapi] — they have mercy on
one another

wakan [wah **kan**] — the sacred, the incomprehensible

Wakan-Tanka [wah **kan** tahn ka] — The Great Mystery,
God

wakinyan [wah **kin** yan] — thunder/lightning beings

Wanbli Gleska [wahn **blee** gleshka] — Spotted Eagle,
symbol of the Great Spirit, Holy Spirit

wasicu [wah **shi** chu] — stranger, white person

wicasa wakan [wee **cha** sha wah **kan**] — holy man,
shaman, conduit for spirits

yuwipi [you **wee** pi] — "they release him," aspect of Lakota religion which uses spirits to perform for the shaman.

The Rites of the Oglala Sioux

The Coming of the
Sacred Pipe — *Canupa Wakan*
[cha **noo** pah **wah** kan]

Keeping/Releasing of
the Soul — [no translation given]

The Rite of Purification — *Inipi* [ee **nee** pee]

Crying for a Vision — *Hanblecheyapi*
[hahn **bleh** chee ya pee]

The Sun Dance — *Wiwanyag Wachipi*
[wee **wahn** yahg
wah **chee** pee]

The Making of Relatives — *Hunkapi* [hoonh **gah** pee]

Preparing for Womanhood — *Ishna Ta Awi Cha Lowan*
[eesh **nah** tah ah wee chah
low an]

The Throwing of the Ball — *Tapa Wakan Yap*
[**tah** pah wah **kan** yahp]

DAY ONE
Meet Kahnigapi

Portrait of Lone Dog

You have to understand an Indian
to see he isn't there
the heavy canvas the blue seizure
of all that could go into it.
...

Only the frame of his face
where the cavalry still moves in a corner
of his mouth. The wagons behind them.
All still....

    —Dakota Indian,
     Lone Dog's Winter Count[1]

Introducing Our Retreat Theme

The task of contemplating and shaping a story about
Nicholas Black Elk as a retreat fell into my hands quite
unexpectedly. What seemed so simple at the beginning
thickened into many complex stories woven into one, my
own included. I cannot deny that many ghosts
accompanied my walk through Black Elk's life and that
finally to tell about his extraordinary life, I had to weave
my own little one in a tiny design along its edges because
his spirit has accompanied me for thirty years.

To invite you into this journey of life (since in the end
our lives will all intertwine) I have chosen the poem

above and the one below to light the way. These poems, written by other Native Americans, express the high and low of Nicholas Black Elk's experience according to my understanding of his interviews and his prayers. "Portrait of Lone Dog" expresses the absence, ("...he isn't there") not only of Black Elk, but of all Native people absent from the non-Indian world of United States history. The 1950's, just after Black Elk died, were the years of my Lakota childhood and adolescence. They were bereft of esteem and respect for my people. But I have lived to see the beginning of a new period in Lakota history, one of empowerment and self-respect. It is from the historical backdrop of Black Elk's life as well as the growth of a healing movement which has awakened our self-respect, esteem and empowerment that our retreat with Black Elk springs.

The second poem expresses in a dawn song of the Guyami, a Central American tribe, a vision of and prayer for wholeness which each morning brings. It reflects the vision of light and life which Black Elk clung to, shared, then never recanted. It is also a way to begin our journey.

Throughout our retreat, the opening and closing prayers are taken from or based on the recorded prayers of Black Elk. His words are indicated in italics. My own adaptations and paraphrases appear in standard type. Occasionally, I have drawn on other Native American spiritual sources.

Opening Prayer

O Wakan-Tanka, Great Spirit of life and resurrection, fill us with the light and hope of your being. Give us strength through your light, to be a relative to all living beings like our brother and friend, Black Elk. And like this....

Song Heard in the Dawn

From the great rock I see it, the Daybreak Star, the
    sign of the dawning.
Above the mountain it rises and my heart dances.
Now the light comes, the light that makes me one
    with all life.
Like the tinamou I am, who sings in the dawn, who
    is humble with love,
Let me be like a ray of light, like a flower blazing
    with light,
Like the waterfall laughing with light, like the great
    tree also,
Mighty in its roots that split the rocks, mighty in its
    head that reaches the sky,
And its leaves catch the light and sing with the wind
    a song of the circle.

Let my life be like the rainbow, whose colors teach
    us unity;
Let me follow always the great circle, the roundness
    of power,
...all the circles of life, and whose command is like
    the thunder:
"Be kind, be kind, be brave, be brave, be pure, be pure,
Be humble as the earth, and be as radiant as the
    sunlight!"
Amen.

                —*Central American Guyami dawn song*[2]

RETREAT SESSION ONE

The communion that Nicholas Black Elk experienced
with the earth and all living beings endures today and

gathers us into itself. The earth was his own relative and as we pray with him we sense that we are related to him and to the earth. To pray with him is to sense a great mystery, *Wakan-Tanka*[3] (God) the elusive presence which defined and shaped his life. We will endeavor to do this with the same purity of heart that he often asked of Wakan-Tanka.

Black Elk was born in 1863 on the Little Powder River in Dakota Territory, now southeast Wyoming. His life began in a Lakota *tioshpaye*[4] (extended family group) of medicine people. Even in that family of several medicine men, chosen people of the spirit world, his childhood name was *Kahnigapi*, meaning "choice"[5] or "they chose him." As a child, he already sensed a call from the *wakan* (sacred) world; of this world we will say more later. His *tioshpaye* hunted in the northwestern reaches of what was accorded the Teton people in the 1851 Fort Laramie Treaty—beyond the Black Hills near Devils Tower in Wyoming.

While he was still a babe in cradleboard, the warriors of his people roundly defeated the United States Cavalry on Montana's Bozeman Trail in a battle called "the Fetterman fight."[6] Like other Teton groups, the Oglala were embroiled in the last great struggle to preserve their nomadic life with its freedom to hunt and follow the buffalo. In the summer of 1875, his people participated in the fateful annihilation of Custer's 7th Cavalry at the Little Big Horn. From then on, the United States government, at the behest of an enraged public, changed its policies from treaty-making to armed muscling of the Plains Indians onto several reservations.

This was the environment in which *Kahnigapi* grew into childhood and young adulthood. Yet, even in the midst of this life-and-death environment, the call from the *wakan* spirit world beckoned and compelled him to respond. At age four, while he played, a voice singing from the other world touched him, but he was too young to understand.[7] When he was five, he received the communication of a kingbird, followed by his first vision. This tiny *hokshila* (boy) understood the bird cautioning him to listen. That quieted him to see two men coming out of the north sky and singing to him:

> Behold him, a sacred voice is calling you.
> All over the sky a sacred voice is calling you.[8]

At nine years of age, while eating at Man Hip's tipi, he heard a spirit voice say: "It is time, now they are calling you." That very evening, he said, "As I came out of the tent both my thighs hurt me."[9] He became mysteriously ill and worsened. He lost consciousness for twelve days. During this twelve-day coma-like period, a great vision of the cosmic completion and fullness of his Lakota world flooded his soul.[10] In it were the powers and directions of the earth and sky: the powerful *wakinyan* (thunder and lightning spirits of the West); the six grandfathers of the Lakota cosmos; the powerful horses of the four directions; the morning star; animal and herb spirits. All spoke to him. He was never the same again and the spirit world's choice of him marked his life to his dying day.

The year 1877 was a tragic one for the Lakota people; government forces began closing in on what had been declared the "off-reservation" northwestern reaches of Teton land.[11] Black Elk's cousin, Crazy Horse, while assenting to imprisonment at Fort Robinson in Nebraska territory, was shot and killed. This frightened Crazy Horse's *tioshpaye*—that of the young Black Elk—and they fled to Canada. While there the *wakinyan* caused the chosen boy to live in constant terror of the thunder beings of his vision and he became obsessed with escaping them. Returning to the United States, his family urged him to seek wisdom through those who had received similar calls, the *wicasa wakan* (the holy men). Thus the remaining years of his youth were given to the discipline of listening to the vision and attempting to deal with it through the guidance of the medicine men of his people. In 1881, at age eighteen, he performed one part of his vision by acting out a huge spectacle of the horse dance at Fort Keough in Wyoming territory.[12] This "reenactment of the *wakan* world" gave him spiritual balance and from that time onward, his people acknowledged him as a chosen *wicasa wakan*, a holy man and healer with power from the spirit world.

The depth and power of that great vision, given completely in Lakota idiom, can only be described as cataclysmic, and Black Elk spent not just his youth, but the remainder of his life discerning its meaning and burden. The vision event itself cast Black Elk into the most profound, supernormal communication with the spirits of all living beings in his Lakota world. But most significant for him was the call he received from the *wakan* world to act and speak on behalf of the people as he relates from his vision:

Then I advanced back to the center where the flowering stick was and the spotted eagle spoke to me saying: "Behold them, these are your people." These little butterflies of all colors seemed to be crying. I could hear them whimpering here and there. The spotted eagle spoke again, saying: "These people shall be in great difficulty and you shall go there." [13]

He was called to be a conduit between the spirit world and his people but in a very special way, as a *heyoka* (sacred clown) or "contrary." "Only those who have had visions of the west, that is to say of the [t]hunder beings [*wakinyan*], can act as *heyokas*."[14] Black Elk would become the fourth generation of his family to serve the *wakan* world in a sacred way, but his call was specified from the spirit of the West. Thus, in sacred public ceremonies, he was to act backward—in a way to make people laugh—so participants would be well disposed to receive the sacred knowledge and truth given in those ceremonies.[15]

Fifty-eight years later, in 1931, Black Elk began to relate the first small portions of his vision to his first editor, John Neihardt.[16] After their first encounter, Neihardt exclaimed to his daughters that what he heard was "like flashes of sheet lightning on a summer night that reveal a strange and beautiful landscape."[17] It was Neihardt who understood the breadth of Black Elk's vision and transcribed it into *Black Elk Speaks*, which would become a world treasure.

Encountering Christianity

By 1886, the year of the Fort Laramie Treaty, twenty-five-year-old Black Elk, tired of the pony-less, circumscribed life of the Pine Ridge Reservation, joined Buffalo Bill's Wild West Show. His first experiences of the East Coast must have been a culture shock. He traveled first to New York City, then to Europe performing for the *wasicus* (white people) of the East Coast and beyond. For three years he traveled with a troupe of Wild West performers acting out what *wasicus* wanted to see: the stories and stereotypes of intrepid pioneers whose progress is impeded by wild Indians.

Though not literate in English, Black Elk was literate in his Lakota dialect and in Europe he managed to write a letter back to his family on the Pine Ridge. In this first letter,[18] he speaks of the child of Imim, an Indian woman in the troupe, who would "receive the law," meaning Baptism. Part of the contract with Buffalo Bill's troupe demanded that each Indian be baptized a Christian. In the troupe, the Episcopal denomination was prominent, so Black Elk "received the law" as part of his early immersion in the *wasicu* world. However, a more indelible part of his entrance into Christianity was his encounter with Jesus Christ and his teachings.

In this same letter, Black Elk writes of another entirely different aspect of the truth for which he hunted his entire life. He wrote a letter while on tour in Europe which was published later in a Presbyterian and Congregational[19] news sheet called *Iapi Oaye*, the *Word Carrier*. In the letter, printed in the December, 1889, issue he wrote in Lakota. What follows is the translation:

> So thus all along, of the white man's many customs, only his faith, the white man's beliefs about God's will, and how they act according to it, I wanted to understand. I traveled to one city after another, and there were many customs around God's will.[20]

Black Elk manifests an extraordinary sensitivity to God's will even when it is expressed in a non-Lakota idiom. He was able to transfer his understanding of the *wakan* from his Lakota religion to what it meant in biblical, literate terms. Describing what he has experienced in the "white man's world" to his relatives who spoke no English whatsoever, his meaning is clear. But, rather than speak of God's will in terms of a song, the sacred horses or one of the grandfather's voices, he writes of the *actions* of the "*wasicu* people...how they act according to it [God's will]..." and [this], he reiterates: "I wanted to understand." It is highly significant, and even surprising, that *wasicu* behavior should be where God's will manifests itself to him, given the recent history of his people's struggle and defeat by the *wasicu* army.

He then goes on in the same letter to quote from

Paul's New Testament writings, mentioning highlights from all the Christian teaching he has heard. It is Paul's famous hymn of charity in 1 Corinthians 13 that attracts him. Noteworthy are the exact words he has chosen, for they could resound in his own great Lakota vision.

> Though I speak with the tongues of men and of angels, and have not charity, I am become as a sounding brass, or a tinkling cymbal. And though I have the gift of prophecy, and understand all mysteries, and all knowledge; and though I have faith, so that I could move mountains, and have not charity, I am nothing. And though I bestow all my goods to feed the poor, and though I give my body to be burned, and have not charity, it profiteth me nothing.[21]

Black Elk's choice of Paul bridges the powerful understanding of the *wakan* from his great vision to the *wasicu* religion. The test of charity, as Paul uses it in this text, is charitable actions or loving, merciful behavior. They in themselves serve as touchstones of the real follower of Christ—the one who knows how to love. There is no Lakota translation for the word "love" or "charity" as Paul refers to it except through *ushimala* (have mercy on me), or *ushikiciyapi* (they have mercy due them on each other).[22]

In another letter, written when he was twenty-five, Black Elk reveals both the rigors of performing with the Wild West Show and his own spiritual discipline during those difficult years.

> Now I will tell you about how I am doing with the wild west show. Always in my mind I hold to the law and all along I live remembering God. But the show runs day and night too, so at two o'clock we quit. But all along I live remembering God so He enables me to do it all.[23]

Although Black Elk left no words to indicate his personal spiritual bond to Jesus Christ from that early period of his life, his 1889 letter from Europe suggests that he did find a link between the teachings of Jesus and his own experience of the *wakan*.[24] The diverse worlds and cultural contexts of Lakota beliefs and Christianity are seen coming together in his quotation of 1 Corinthians 13. His use of this quotation and his commentary on it, appear to unite these worlds within him around his understanding of charity, the very heart and center of Christian teachings. It points to Black Elk's recognition that the manifestation of "charity" of the New Testament is the same as fulfilling "God's will," or the will of *Wakan-Tanka*.

This connection further resounds in Paul's self-effacing "only boast of my weakness" (1 Corinthians 13:5). As with all traditional Lakota, when Black Elk speaks of his communication with the sacred he uses the words "sending a pitiful voice." His prayer always accentuates his own existential weakness and that of human beings who are *ushica* (in a miserable state of being, either spiritually or materially). The Lakota verb from the same root is *ushimala* (take pity on me). The root *ushi-* has no exact translation into English, except as love or compassion[25] given to one who desperately needs help.

Black Elk's 1889 letter underlines his appreciation of how white people knew how to carry out God's will—because God's will was of central importance to him. In the biblical term *charity* (agape or compassion), we sense a bridge through which Black Elk could recognize and identify with his own understanding of *ushica*. Shortly after he wrote this letter, he returned to his reservation home just before the final diminishment of his people.

The Ghost Dance: A Revival

By 1900, government policy had effectively suppressed all forms of the cultural and spiritual life of Native Americans. A Christian Indian man of the Northern Paiute, Wovoka, began to pray for a solution to this situation. His prayers led him to a vision of the Indian messiah who would come and bring new life to the Indians. Black Elk understood the messiah as the Wanekia, from *wanikiya*, meaning "Makes live."[26]

Ghost Dancing was part of a pan-Indian religious movement that was sweeping across the Western Plains. Returning to Pine Ridge, Black Elk could not ignore its importance for his people. For those who had experienced the tragic diminishment of their lives, the dance helped them to deal with consternation and grief.[27]

Though he at first resisted joining the Ghost Dance,[28] Black Elk's reputation as a *wicasa wakan* made him a sought-after leader. This is, no doubt, the reason why the Brule on the Rosebud reservation invited him to come and lead their Ghost Dancing. His spirituality found a place in the movement from the time he entered it; he possessed the power to incite visions in Ghost Dancers he led. Black Elk related that when he held up the red flowering stick of his vision among the Rosebud, they began to fall to the ground with visions.[29] For him, the Ghost Dance was an attempt to revive Lakota life and spirit. The nomadic life—the buffalo-hunting culture at the center of Lakota traditional life—had ended. Black Elk's own Ghost Dance vision of the Wanekia, or *wanikiya*, tells us about early reservation existence which needed revival. Disillusionment with *wasicu* policies and desperation to escape them was a common experience among all traditional Teton of that time.

But the revival of Lakota spirit through the Ghost

Dance died with the 7th Cavalry's massacre of Minneconjou and Hunkpapa Lakotas at Wounded Knee on December 30, 1890. Black Elk told of his failed attempt to use his spiritual power to rescue the Lakota people from the soldiers at Wounded Knee. Instead, he was hit by a bullet. At the end of his account of this period he simply said: "Two years later I got married."[30]

Black Elk married twice and outlived both of his wives. His first wife, of a Lakota traditional marriage, was Katie War Bonnet who bore him three boys, two of whom died in childhood: William died in infancy in 1895 and John died in 1909 of tuberculosis, a disease widespread among Northern Plains tribes in the early reservation period. Katie War Bonnet died in 1901. Black Elk's daughter Lucy relates that he married the second time to her mother, Anna Brings White—a widow with two children, Mary and Agatha. Lucy, his only daughter, and Nicholas, Jr., were children of that marriage. However, Lucy tells that her two half-sisters also died of tuberculosis. At the end of his life Black Elk had buried two wives and four children taken by illness in those early days on the Pine Ridge.[31]

In the years of his married life, Black Elk experienced the havoc caused by government attempts to assimilate the Oglala. It was in this period after Wounded Knee that the severe social and economic challenges of assimiliation faced them daily. The oppression of the Oglala culture, its social structures and spiritual rituals took full effect on the Pine Ridge.[32] Though Black Elk continued to serve his people as a *yuwipi* man, we hear nothing of his great vision during this time; it was eclipsed by the dark reality of events. Yet it was precisely during this dark night that Black Elk's immense spiritual resources came into play.

Encountering Catholicism

The resiliency of Black Elk's spiritual genius emerged during this time. His people had been pushed violently into a historic period for which there was no comparison, no reference point to prepare them for such catastrophic changes. Almost overnight their free, nomadic, self-directed existence became a life hedged in geographically, restricted at every level to the confines of the reservation. Following the Wounded Knee massacre, from 1890 to 1904, Black Elk continued to follow his Lakota spiritual calling through the practice of *yuwipi* and Indian medicine, calling forth his power figures in the spirit world. In this way, he served as a healer among his people in those early reservation years.

It is precisely during this dark period when the strengths inherent in the Lakota culture of life took shape in him. Black Elk was part of the generation forced "to create their own patterns of behavior."[33] In this task, unnamed by any previous experience, he drew wisdom from his Lakota traditions. That background gave him the central way of perceiving himself as one who was interconnected with all living beings of the earth. This deeply rooted awareness sprang from centuries of lived experience of the Northern Plains Indians: It was at the core of their self-definition and understanding.

Further, the economic and social underpinnings of Lakota life sprang from this profound conviction of *Mitakuye Oyasin*, "all beings are my relatives" or, "I am connected to all creation." Human goodness was achieved by being a good relative to all his relations.

Another quality which Black Elk inherited from his people was an ability to adapt to new circumstances and situations. The nomadic life gave the Lakota people a willingness to negotiate many changes of environment and place. And these qualities—the sense of relatedness and adaptability—found their source, strength and resilience in the way they lived with the supernatural.[34] For them, *Wakan-Tanka* and the world of spirits was the ultimate source of their spiritual power. The hunting culture of the Great Plains tribes forged Black Elk into a human being totally given over to the reality of the *wakan*, the world of *Wakan-Tanka*, the great mysterious presence which contained all the powers of the earth in one. It is not possible to know exactly how Black Elk transferred these basic spiritual tenets and understanding of *wakan* to the Catholic Church; we only know that he did so in an unprecedented way.

In November of 1904[35] the meaning of his vision took another turn when he was baptized into the Catholic Church by Father Ledebner, S.J. He was given a new name, Nicholas (because he entered the Church on December 6, the feast of Saint Nicholas), which he kept the remainder of his life.[36]

We can only imagine what a cataclysmic change this was for him, moving away from the earth-based, nonliterate spiritual experiences which flooded his consciousness in his vision and its consequent *yuwipi* and Indian medicine. From that familiar setting he moved into a highly structured, literate Church where creed and doctrine were primary.

Yet Black Elk's inner vision, belied by his physical near-blindness, enabled him to integrate these diverse worlds through his understanding of the *wakan* and through the meaning of *ushica*. In the new reservation life he recognized the *wasicu* place of the sacred; it drew him and made sense to him. Perhaps his gift of immense spiritual sensitivity opened a way for him to recognize *wakan* when it was manifested within another, very different socio-religious context.

What was not alien to him was his belief in *Wakan-Tanka* as the one God. Nicholas Black Elk found meaning in the grim recent events that led to reservation life only through his resignation to the will of *Wakan-Tanka*. In plain terms, this meant Black Elk perceived these historic events as a possible expression of God's will.

There is evidence to support Black Elk's acceptance of Catholicism within his own spiritual calling, the place of *wakan*. There he was at home, for he had learned to evoke the sacred in order to be its conduit. By nature, he was drawn to the beauty of sacred liturgy. His experience of ritual and symbol in the Lakota world was highly developed before he entered the Church, and the liturgy of the Roman Catholic Church at that time was highly structured and often elaborately celebrated. The celebration of Mass used *wakan* persons, clothing, language, space, ritual movements, objects and songs. So also, the *wakan* was evoked in Lakota religious practice through sacred persons, in sacred ritual, language and objects. Ritual and ceremony were Black Elk's home territory; they were understandable when perhaps creed and catechism were not.

Witness to his respect for the Mass is given by Jesuit Father Sialm, who relates that in Oglala, South Dakota, on the Feast of Corpus Christi, 1923, Black Elk dressed in traditional costume and led other dancers in a procession to honor the *"Yutapi Wakan,"* the Sacred Bread of the altar.[37] This shows that Black Elk had accomplished his own type of theological processing; his actions speak louder than words.

Further, the structured community life, endurance and longevity of the missionary priests, brothers and sisters at Holy Rosary Mission near Manderson, South Dakota presented a way of life similar to that of the *tioshpaye*. Often, long-term friendships with these missionaries deepened the meaning of the Catholic faith for Black Elk as the "charity, love" of his 1886 letter.

Importantly, the move into the Catholic Church gave Black Elk's family a way to subsist economically during one of the lowest ebbs of Lakota life. Thus, being Catholic provided a means of survival in early reservation life. Early on he was recruited as a catechist. This provided employment among his people in an area familiar to him—the life of communion with the *wakan*, although now it was filtered through to him in translation from the Roman Catholic Church. A 1935 photograph shows Black Elk as a catechist instructing children with a Two Roads map—a picture catechism illustrating salvation history.

Along with the ritual life, the St. Mary and St. Joseph Societies provided a framework reminiscent of one of the strongest features of his culture. These societies had structured the Lakota nomadic life and helped it to thrive and develop socially.[38] Through the formation of these two Catholic societies among the Lakota, Catholic missionaries strengthened what was familiar to the Lakota before Christianity. The various Lakota societies, *okolakiciyapi*,[39] of the pre-Christian days glued the bands together by enhancing a sense of social belonging, self-esteem and achievement.

The St. Joseph Society gave Black Elk visibility among his people and enabled him to grow as spiritual leader and prayer healer within a Catholic setting. In this way he was able to adapt to the enormous change demanded of him. So, he carried on his life as family man and Oglala leader in a diminished Oglala society with energy, intelligence and commitment to the Catholic Church. His entry into the Church paralleled that of many other Oglala. His daughter Lucy spoke of it in this way:

After the Jesuits baptized several in each district,

they pretty soon began to get men like my father to
be catechists. In every station they appointed two or
three catechists to work with the people. These
laymen were trained to conduct services, read
Scripture on Sundays, baptize if necessary, visit the
sick, and bury the dead. But most of all, they were
trained to teach the Catholic faith.[40]

Thus, he continued to serve his people as he had been
called to do in his great vision, though in an entirely
different milieu and not without the humor of his *heyoka*
spirit.

To illustrate Black Elk's humanity, there are stories
told by Lucy about comic incidents during his catechist
days. One of them relates how he and Father Grotegeers
rode on a motorcycle to an Oglala village on the Pine
Ridge Reservation to hold services there. When they
arrived at the church, the Jesuit could not stop the
motorcycle, so he turned it toward the race track. Still
unable to stop the machine after several laps, they headed
back to the mission. En route, Father Grotegeers decided
to stop the motorcycle by running into a bank. This story
caused merriment in Black Elk's family when Black Elk
said to the priest, "You nearly killed me!"

There is another story of how Black Elk, nearly blind,
donned his wife's high-shouldered coat by accident and
went off to church services, unaware of his mistake. After
he finished preaching, one of the men commented on his
nice coat. Lucy says her father got mad at her mother,
telling her to hang her coat somewhere else.

In 1929, John Neihardt (then poet laureate of
Nebraska) came to Black Elk seeking information from an
Indian elder for his epic poetry of the Old West; he had
no notion of the man he was to encounter. He relates that
as he arrived at Black Elk's home in Manderson, it
appeared as though Black Elk were waiting for him and

showed no surprise at his arrival. Later, he confided to Neihardt that indeed a spirit had led him (Neihardt) there to hear of his great vision. From these first translated and transcribed interviews Neihardt published *Black Elk Speaks*.

In 1944, Neihardt visited Black Elk once again to learn about the stories and myths of the Lakota worldview. The results of this encounter were published in a book called *When the Tree Flowered*. After this interview, Nicholas Black Elk maintained that he had given all of his power over to Neihardt by relating his great vision in its entirety—for the power of his vision lay in its telling. Yet there was another great publication still to come.

In 1947, John Neihardt dictated a letter to Black Elk recommending Joseph Epes Brown, a young student of anthropology from Indiana University. He wrote that this was a "...fine young man whose interest in religious and spiritual matters was sincere."[41] In 1947 and 1948 Joseph E. Brown lived two years with the family of Black Elk taking notes and learning about Lakota ritual and ceremony directly from the old man himself. From those interviews, Nicholas Black Elk made his final contribution to the world in *The Sacred Pipe: Black Elk's Account of the Seven Rites of the Oglala Sioux*.[42] It is a book of ritual and includes source stories of how the ceremonies came to be tradition among the Lakota. Within two years after dictating this final work, on August 17, 1950, Nicholas Black Elk died in his home after receiving the last rites, Extreme Unction and Holy Viaticum. He was a faithful Catholic and true Lakota to the end.

Our Retreat Goal

Nicholas Black Elk's great vision dominated his consciousness and memory throughout his life. Yet, in a way, the vision was given to all human beings. Our task in this retreat is to look at the evidence of Black Elk's life as a spiritual quest and try to understand what he saw many years ago as *Kahnigapi* (the chosen one). In entering this retreat we, too, cry out from our hearts and "send our voices" skyward asking for a vision which will lead us through our own tumultuous times.

For Reflection

- *Reflect upon the life of this man and his different names: Kahnigapi, Hehaka Sapa, Nicholas Black Elk: What in Black Elk's life is most noteworthy for you? Is there a similar event in your own life?*

- *In retrospect, what can we see perhaps better than he could about the meaning of his life? What are we not yet able to perceive about his life?*

- *Do you find episodes in Black Elk's life that resonate with your own experiences? How are they similar?*

Closing Prayer

Black Elk's daughter, Lucy Looks Twice, sang the first song her father ever taught her. Let us listen to this prayer and join in with our own.

Knowing what we know about Black Elk, we close this day with the following song-prayer.

Wakantanka lila waste
  Slolyeic iya cin ce;
    Oyas tanyan iyuskin po,
    Niucantepi nicila.
    Lakota oniyatepi,
  Koyan ekta up ye;
Jesus niyuhapi kta ce
    Heon oyas nicopi.

O God most good
    Who wants to make himself known,
    All rejoice rightly,
He asks of you your hearts.
    You Lakota are a nation,
Quickly may they come together;
    Jesus would have it so,
    Because he has called you all.[43]

O *Wakan-Tanka*, Great Mysterious One! You are the source
and end of everything. My Father, Wakan-Tanka, you are
the one who watches over and sustains all life.

O My Grandmother! You are the earthly source of all
existence and Mother Earth. The fruits which you bear are
the source of life for the earth peoples. You are watching
over your fruits as does a mother. May the steps which
we take upon you during this retreat be sacred and not
weak! Amen.

Notes

1 Diane Glancy, *Lone Dog's Winter Count* (Albuquerque, N.M.: West End Press, 1991).

2 Vinson Brown, *Voices of Earth and Sky: The Vision Life of the Native Americans* (Happy Camp, Calif.: Naturegraph Publishers, Inc., 1976), p. 13.

3 *Wakan-Tanka* rather than *Wakantanka* which he used when translating the word for God. Raymond DeMallie.

4 This Lakota term describes the family group: *oshpaye* + *ti* (dwelling or house, as a *tipi*). It is the basic organization block in Lakota nomadic society.

5 Raymond J. DeMallie, ed. and intro., *The Sixth Grandfather: Black Elk's Teachings Given to John G. Neihardt* (Lincoln, Neb.: University of Nebraska Press, Bison paperback, 1985, first published 1984), p. 5. From the original stenographic notes of *Black Elk Speaks* and *When the Tree Flowered*.

6 See George E. Hyde, *Red Cloud's Folk: A History of the Oglala Sioux Indians* (Norman, Okla.: University of Oklahoma Press, 1979).

7 DeMallie, p. 108.

8 DeMallie, p. 109.

9 DeMallie, p. 111.

10 DeMallie, pp. 111-112, and Hilda Neihardt, *Black Elk and Flaming Rainbow: Personal Memories of the Lakota Holy Man and John Neihardt* (Lincoln, Neb.: University of Nebraska Press, 1995), pp. 50-72.

11 *Annual Report of the Commissioner of Indian Affairs to the Secretary of the Interior for the Year 1877* (Washington: Government Printing Office, 1878). The letter from an agent of Dakota territory specifies the extent to which the Sioux are to be stripped of central accoutrements of their culture: tipi poles, colored cloth, blankets, paint, ponies. Passes given to people for inter-reservation travel were severely restricted, most passes meant attendance at ceremonies, especially death rites for relatives on other reservations.

12 DeMallie, pp. 215-235.

13 DeMallie, pp. 228-229.

14 DeMallie, pp. 232-233.

15 DeMallie, p. 232.

16 From these original interviews, Neihardt edited and published *Black Elk Speaks*. The material for this retreat book is taken from the original untransliterated stenographic notes of 1931 and 1944.

These are contained in *The Sixth Grandfather*, as primary source.

[17] Neihardt, *Black Elk and Flaming Rainbow*, p. 16.

[18] DeMallie, p. 7.

[19] DeMallie, pp. 8-9.

[20] DeMallie, p. 10.

[21] 1 Corinthians 13.

[22] Eugene Beuchel, S.J., *Lakota-English Dictionary* (Red Cloud Indian School, 1972), p. 398.

[23] DeMallie, p. 8.

[24] DeMallie, p. 10. In the same letter, Black Elk speaks of Jesus "whom the *wasicu*s killed across the ocean." He expresses a desire to visit the land of Jesus, to see it for himself and be able to tell his relatives about it.

[25] *Ushikiciyapi* (they have "compassionate love"). Translation by Ben Black Bear, Jr.

[26] DeMallie, p. 266.

[27] The period following the Wounded Knee massacre was socially and psychologically catastrophic for Black Elk and his peers.

[28] For a fuller account, see DeMallie, pp. 256-269. Black Elk's people urged him to become involved, because he was known as a spiritual leader.

[29] DeMallie, p. 266.

[30] DeMallie, p. 282.

[31] Michael F. Steltenkamp, *Black Elk: Holy Man of the Oglala* (Norman, Okla.: University of Oklahoma Press, 1993), p. 18. Lucy Looks Twice, daughter of Black Elk, relates her memories of her father as a Catholic catechist.

[32] For an account of the Sun Dance during the Ban Period (1883-1934/1952), see Clyde Holler, *Black Elk's Religion: The Sun Dance and Lakota Catholicism* (Syracuse, N.Y.: Syracuse University Press, 1995).

[33] Steltenkamp, p. 10.

[34] Steltenkamp, p. 12.

[35] Steltenkamp, pp. 33-35.

[36] Steltenkamp, Chapter 3.

[37] Steltenkamp, p. 80; DeMallie, p. 25.

[38] Royal B. Hassrick, *Civilization of the American Indian Series, Vol. 72, The Sioux: Life and Customs of a Warrior Society* (Norman, Okla.: University of Oklahoma Press, 1964).

[39] Frances Densmore, *Bureau of Ethnology Bulletin Series*, Vol. 61,

Sioux Music, (San Diego: Parmer Books, 1918).

[40] Steltenkamp, p. 50.

[41] Neihardt, p. 114.

[42] *Civilization of the American Indian Series, Vol. 36* (Norman, Okla.: University of Oklahoma Press, 1988, first published in 1953). Used extensively in preparing this retreat.

[43] Steltenkamp, p. 50.

DAY TWO

The Sacred Hoop
Black Elk's World

"...I remember Black Elk's words: "You can just look around you and see that it is true!"[1]

Coming Together in the Spirit

"Just look around you and see...." This sounds like a simple exhortation but life has taught me that it is not simple at all. If someone had said forty years ago that one day I would be telling the story of Black Elk and praying with him, disbelief would have frozen my face into a patronizing smile. Thoughts like this remind me that sometimes the most difficult people to lead to truth are the ones who already think they are right or, worse yet, *know* they are right.

At one time, I had no doubt that I was right about Indian religion, Indian medicine, Lakota philosophy and life-ways. My brother recently reminded me of the evenings we spent arguing about the validity of Lakota religion and medicine. Of course, I never strayed from the true teaching of the Catholic Church and still have not, but only understand it—and life—more deeply. When my brother and I parted ways, we agreed to disagree and promised prayers for each other. His prayers for me have been answered because my understanding and respect for the ways of my ancestors has grown and so has respect for myself and my people. Black Elk's teaching has been a great part of that transformation.

It took me many years to "look around me and see" that Indian people all across this country were becoming sane, coming to their senses, sobering up, experiencing healing and health by returning to the old ways. In those years, I also did my own research, study and prayer into the truth which I proclaimed back then. After seven years of study at the font of Catholic teaching in Rome (the Gregorian Biblicum), I returned humbled, realizing that true knowledge cannot be gained by reading all the books in the world. Rather, wisdom begins to grow when you "look around you and see."

Defining Our Thematic Context

In maturing, I've learned that the truth, for me, lies in the union of the Lakota ways and the Catholic faith. In our modern world, often we find truth by passing through profound spiritual, social, cultural and economic displacement. I write from that uncomfortable place, where millions of the globe's inhabitants are thrust now, with no secure home, no freedom to live according to their cultural heritage. The prayers of this retreat cry out from the discomfort of displacement, as have the prayers of my people for five hundred years. Where is the truth of our humanity? With this eternal question let us enter the second day of our retreat with Black Elk.

Opening Prayer

"My grandfather, the Great Spirit, you are the only one and to no other can anyone send voices. They have said you have made everything. The four quarters crossing each other

you have made...."[2] Wakan-Tanka, we stand at the edge of a new world era. You are the only one who gives us humans true understanding. I am blind...like a poor beggar in the desert—at the beginning of a journey into God. Have pity on me as I stand here crying for a vision. Give me a vision, O Great Spirit! I cannot hear the movements and sounds of what lies ahead unless you open my inner ears. My heart is numb to the stark realities which face us today as a global people. You are the source of all enlightenment and spiritual wisdom. Bless this my time of retreat. Give me compassion, your compassion which reaches around, above, below and throughout all creation, so that one day I and all human beings, may live in right relationship with all living beings—two-legged, four-legged, winged creatures and those who live in water—all over this globe. Amen.

RETREAT SESSION TWO

For those who spend most of their lives in civilized settings which are both climate-controlled and tidy, praying with Black Elk means entering another way of being. This "way of being" is the world of the circle, or the hoop of life, in which the myriad forms of life on this earth and under the sky are related and interdependent: the two-legged, the four-legged, the winged ones and those that live in the water. In the Lakota world and the world of Native American spiritual traditions, all are perceived and named as *relatives*. The Lakota universe is the world of the *Sacred* Hoop, *wakan* because the wealth of life dwells in the hoop or circle of the earth surrounding us. We creatures of the earth all share this life; it has been *given* as gift to all of us. We are related. The living, breathing life of Nicholas Black Elk was the dynamic reality that related him to all beings. Despite a life of dramatic events this was his primary state of being and this he *shared* with all living beings. It

"...grew out of the thoughts of people who lived close to the earth, who could and did look about themselves and see that they, all living things, and the earth they called Mother were part of a vast system that included in its mystery the winds, the sun, the moon, and the stars. I listened...we all did...with rapt attention and felt that power in his words as Black Elk told about this great hoop."[3]

Hilda Neihardt, witness to the 1931 and 1944 interviews with Black Elk, believes that the Native American people may not have been as technologically advanced as the Europeans, but "they were developed in other important ways," especially in the awareness that the world and its creatures cannot exist outside of interdependence. It's a simple concept, but one that our splintered, distracted consciousness has lost sight of and grasps only with difficulty. When you begin to sense this truth, you will enter Black Elk's way of being.

"And that is the sacred hoop. The power for everything an Indian does comes from the sacred hoop, and the power will not work in anything but a circle. Everything now is too square. The sacred hoop is vanishing among the people."[4]

The hoop of life is gathered and held in place by *Skan*, the name for the sky, together with *Unci Maka*, the name for Grandmother Earth. But the sky is imaged as containing all the powers because it symbolizes *Wakan-Tanka*. When we begin to pray within the sacred hoop, our prayers are lifted or sung toward *Skan* and toward *Wanbli Gleska*, the spotted eagle who dwells in the deep heavens and images the Holy Spirit. Both *Skan* and *Wanbli Gleska* symbolize the vast, incomprehensible One which most humans name variously as "God." Sometimes during Lakota ceremonies an eagle will appear soaring overhead or other birds will fly in and perch nearby. Black Elk would say they are your relatives and they want to join your prayer to *Wakan-Tanka*.

Completing the powerful circle of life is our relative without whom we could neither walk nor stand: *Unci Maka*, Grandmother Earth.

Earth is your grandmother and mother,[5] and She is sacred. Every step that is taken upon her should be as a prayer.[6]

The sky, earth and four directions form the Sacred Hoop and the ritual background upon which our retreat with Black Elk takes place. Whenever Lakota refer to their universe in a ceremonial way, they say *Mitakuye Oyasin*, "All my relatives." It is both a salutation of respect and honor as well as an affirmation of the Lakota reality of this universe.

Across this great hoop of life there are two roads: the Red Road, running North and South, which crosses the center of the Black Road running East and West. We all know these roads. The Black Road begins in the East where human beings are born and ends in the West where light disappears. This is the road of problems, heartaches, anguish and tragedy which we all walk. In describing the way of the Black Road, our retreat director understates his belief about life:

Black Elk thought a bit and then explained: "It is not easy to live in this world."[7]

If our journey through life were only upon the Black Road, there would be no reason to live, but we have been given also the Red Road of *spiritual understanding*:

"It begins in the [S]outh where lives the power to grow and proceeds to the [N]orth, the region of white hairs and death."[8]

Where these two roads cross is the center of the sacred hoop; their juncture is the dynamic center—the heart—of each human being.

The Center[9]

When Black Elk prayed as a Lakota he always began with the earth, at the center of the directions.[10] In all the Lakota ceremonies, Black Elk reiterated the importance of the center. In the Sun Dance, the sacredness of the center was expressed through the tree at the center of the dance circle. Black Elk named the circle the *hoop*[11] of the people and at the center of it stood the cottonwood tree, rich symbol of life. It represented spiritual balance at the center of the directions where *Wakan-Tanka* dwells. At that tree, when dancers tore their flesh and shed blood, it was a symbolic act done in honor and gratitude in the presence of the Great Mysterious One. In most Sun Dances, the cottonwood was cut down the day before; in this ritual, the people gathered around in respect for the tree because it was about to give its life for them. It was honored just as veterans who have given their lives for their people.

In the Releasing of the Soul ceremony,[12] the belongings of the deceased person were placed in a tree at the center of the ritual area—the most sacred place. After a year of being kept, the soul was purified and journeyed South but still dwelled at the center, both of the ritual circle and of the people. Because of this, the purified soul at the tree in the center of the hoop continued to thrive like a tree in bloom. The prayer of the leader was: *"The Sacred influence of your son's soul will be upon the people; it is as a tree that will always bloom."*[13] The soul was a spiritual reality at the root of the *wakan tree* in the center of the nation's hoop.[14] In combining the human soul with the tree metaphor, Black Elk awakened the image of the dance circle, metaphorically the "hoop of the people."

To place oneself at the center and to remain there, then, was a critical and profoundly spiritual process for Black Elk. All else, even the Lakota rituals themselves, could never happen without first establishing the Center.[15] At the close of the Sun Dance, the following instruction was given to the dancers:

By your actions today you have strengthened the sacred hoop of our nation. You have made a sacred center which will always be with you, and you have created a sacred relationship with all things of the universe.[16]

The importance of the center in Black Elk's thought is deepened further in his explanation of the *Hunkapi*, the ceremony to make new relatives.[17] *"In this rite we establish a relationship on earth which is reflective of that real relationship which exists between man and Wakan-Tanka."*[18]

If you wish to pray as he did then you also must establish a center and prepare to "send your voice" from that center. This is the ceremonial attitude and the proper respectful manner to adopt in the presence of *Wakan-Tanka*. To Black Elk, the sacredness of God's presence demanded a structured, ritual approach, and the first step to enter this presence was to prepare a place as the center of the four directions. It is exactly there, as he learned from his ancestors, that *Wakan-Tanka* is manifested in your own Sacred Hoop "where you live, move and have your being."

For Black Elk it was never a question of where and how to pray, because for him and his people of the great northern plains the earth oriented its power in given ways. He prayed in the seven directions: Zenith (Sky), Nadir (Earth), North, East, South and West, and last, he prayed for spiritual power within his own weak self. Black Elk learned that whoever found a center also became the center of the universe and that is where God dwells.[19] By placing himself at this center which was simultaneously physical, spiritual and metaphorical, he encountered the Great Mysterious One. Whenever or wherever he stood in an attitude of respect at this center within and without, that moment was the proper time to "send a voice." Then *the center of oneself becomes the center of the universe. The center of the earth and the center of the person are one and the same.* For Black Elk, earth, in its essence, was not only a physical reality but a spiritual reality. Therefore, making a prayer with your feet on the earth is doubly real and binding.

"...*It is very sacred, for we have here established the center of earth, and this center, which is in reality everywhere, is the home, the dwelling place of Wakan-Tanka.*"[20]

Black Elk and his Lakota ancestors learned from the earth itself that you approach *Wakan-Tanka* through the sacred directions and you throw your voice and being out from the center. *Mitakuye Oyasin,* "all my relatives," with all beings and creatures of the world, I shall be as a relative.

The Lakota Virtues

In this retreat we will follow the rhythm of the earth and sky by focusing on one of the four directions each day. To enrich the retreat, we will follow the four Lakota virtues or values: humility, wisdom, generosity and courage. When I sought the written document or source of these virtues, Black Elk's great-granddaughter, Charlotte Black Elk[21] told me that these virtues have been held by our Lakota people since time began. I present them to you as valuable Lakota oral tradition. Experience and observation teaches the learner that these virtues have characterized many Native Americans, especially

Black Elk. To engage in his prayers one senses the heart of a man who knew who he was in God's presence; this is *humility*. In the later years of his life, Black Elk and his family prepared a traditional Giveaway and Feast to honor John Neihardt and his daughters.[22] Later, at the Neihardts' 1931 departure:

The next day, May 29, the Neihardts loaded their car with the painted tipi cover and many other presents from their friends in Manderson and headed for the Black Hills.[23]

That such a poor family could give "many presents" to Neihardt and his daughters is notable. Such gestures have always characterized Lakota society which holds *generosity* as a common value. Many tribal people respect elders for their *wisdom*. This has grown in contemporary ritual and social practice among all urban and reservation Indians. *Courage* and bravery have been the central virtues and values of Lakota culture through the last hundred years. In our retreat, we will blend the virtues with each of the four directions to enrich our prayer with Black Elk. According to Lakota custom, praying from the center yields balance. This balance then flowers forth in acts of habitual goodness which make us become better human beings.

For Reflection

- *As Black Elk did, you must place your being—body, mind, inner spirit—at the center of the world. For him "...this center is really everywhere, it is within each of us..." but its reality is embodied in this world, on the earth.*

- *Look around the place of your retreat and locate the spot where you wish to spend your time praying with Black Elk. Unless it is impossible for you, it would be best to find a quiet place outdoors.*

- *Quietly and prayerfully decide what your center will be. Remember, the center is mainly within yourself. If you cannot find an ideal place, understand that you can pray anywhere and still be at the center.*

- *Prepare an altar or place a symbol there representing your center. Or, carry a symbol of your center with you each day to the place of your prayer.*

- *In this retreat, stand upon the earth, slowly turn around facing each direction in turn. Throw your voice and your spirit out from the center of the Sacred Hoop of your retreat. Just be there.*

- *Spend time quieting yourself, then in stillnes watch for your relatives—the other creatures of the earth—around you. Which relative will accompany you on this retreat? Invite that relative to join you as you enter Black Elk's world.*

Closing Prayer

O Grandfather, *Wakan-Tanka*, I shall now make this your sacred place. In making this altar, all the birds of the air and all creatures of the earth will rejoice, and they will come from all directions to behold it! All the generations of my people will rejoice! This place will be the center of the paths of your four great Powers. The dawn of the day will see this holy place! When your light approaches, O *Wakan-Tanka*, all that moves in the universe will rejoice. *Mitakuye Oyasin!*

Notes

[1] Neihardt, p. 61.

[2] DeMallie, p. 237.

[3] Neihardt, pp. 57-58.

[4] Neihardt, p. 59.

[5] *Civilization of the American Indian Series, Vol. 36* Joseph Epes Brown, ed. and recorder, *The Sacred Pipe: Black Elk's Account of the Seven Rites of the Oglala Sioux*, (Norman, Okla.: University of Oklahoma Press, 1989, first published 1953), p. 6. Three years before his death, Black Elk spent two years with Joseph E. Brown relating his understanding of the Oglala ceremonies. The earth's presence as mother can be experienced in the "...*act* of power which produces, nurtures, gives and nurtures life." [sic] Her presence as grandmother is understood with the *potency* or the potential and power of life to continue as the "ground and substance of all things...and all that can be or can yet come."

[6] Brown, pp. 5-6.

[7] Hilda Neihardt, *The Sacred Hoop* (Tekamah, Neb.: Neihardt!, 1993), p. 2. Hilda Neihardt's memories of Black Elk's teaching with symbols, animals and colors.

[8] Neihardt, *The Sacred Hoop*, p. 3.

[9] The notion of the center as it is used in this retreat is derived from its many references in Brown's *The Sacred Pipe*. In each of the seven rituals establishing the center is of key importance and consequence. How you situate the center—in a holy manner, at a place in reference to the directions—is crucial.

[10] Brown, pp. 108, 109.

[11] Neihardt, *When the Tree Flowered* (Lincoln, Neb.: University of Nebraska Press, 1991).

[12] Brown, "Ritual for Releasing of the Soul."

[13] Brown, p. 29.

[14] Brown, p. 27.

[15] To remain at this center one can be in a threefold peace: peace within oneself with Wakan-Tanka, peace between individuals and, last, the peace between nations. In the Hunkapi (the Making of Relatives ceremony), Black Elk reiterates at the conclusion of the ceremony that the central goal of the ceremony is to establish this threefold peace. But the first peace—the most important from which all other peace flows—is that which comes in the souls of human beings. This peace does not come unless they realize that at the center of the universe dwells Wakan-Tanka. He concludes:

"...This is the real Peace, [sic] and the others are but reflections of this."

[16] Brown, p. 100.

[17] Brown, Chapter 4.

[18] Brown, p. 101.

[19] Black Elk shares this knowledge with many great mystics of the world. The holiest place is where Wakan-Tanka dwells. When you consciously stand at the center of the directions you become that center because God dwells there and then, within you.

[20] Brown, p. 108. Make no mistake about it, this is the same attitude Black Elk took on—in the presence of God. If you desire to pray with Black Elk, then you must assume, as he did, that only the holy or the sacred dimension will give meaning to your life.

[21] A great-grandchild of Nicholas Black Elk who lives in Manderson, South Dakota.

[22] Brown, p. 115. Also, to embody this truth and express the need for cleansing, Lakota purify themselves in the sweatlodge and prepare the immediate physical environment and surroundings with deliberation within the directions.

[23] Brown, p. 115.

DAY THREE

The North: "The Great Purifier"
Humility

"O You, Power, where the Giant lives:
You are a relative."[1]

Coming Together in the Spirit

Kemo Sabe

In my dream I take
the white man
slap him
til he loves me.
I tie him to the house
take his land
& buffalo.
I put other words
into his mouth
words he doesn't understand
like spoonfuls
of smashed lima beans
until his cheeks
bulge.
Chew now, dear
I say.
I flick his throat until he swallows.
He works all day

never leaves the house.
The floors shine
the sheets are starched.
He wipes the grime
from the windows
until clouds dance
across the glass.
He feeds me
when I'm hungry.
I can leave whenever
I want.
Let him struggle
for his dignity
this time
let him remember
my name.
 — *Diane Glancy*[2]

The poem above is written hard with narrow design; it crystallizes human rage. Not just the rage of Native American/Indian people, but of all people who have experienced oppression. Vengeance is a well-known desire; instinctively, we return word for word, blow for blow to those who have hurt or offended us. This is the true violence in human affairs, always seeking entrance at the center of our hearts. Therefore, we must hold revenge and other dark emotions carefully, that they may be purified as we face the North.

  Dark movements of the heart such as jealousy, lust, rage, sloth and pride are compressed within our heart's space. They frequently are caused by suffering inflicted on us. Even as the poem above—out of balance, one-sided—they twist the human heart, weigh it down, push it out of balance with all life. When these movements are empowered by our actions and unleashed into our lives, the results can be more destructive than winter blizzards with treacherous winds. When people act from such a twisted inner state of pain and darkness, their actions leave pain, disease and destruction, in their wake. Black Elk knew this very well. Just as spiritual respect for the powers of the earth formed his consciousness, he was also conscious of such dark movements of the heart, seeking to cleanse them, to stand with pure heart before Wakan-Tanka.

Defining Our Thematic Context

As we begin our third day of retreat we open ourselves to Black Elk's understanding of the North, the direction of purification. Purification is not an option in Lakota ritual, it is demanded. Each ceremony began with the *inipi* (sweatlodge) facing the North. On this day we will reflect on the meaning of purification not just of the earth but of the human heart.

Opening Prayer

O Great Spirit, "...*through the power of the spirit in the [N]orth we are now making ourselves pure and clean, leaving all impure thoughts and ignorance...to become as children newly born.*"[3] Cleanse us of all hatred and vindictiveness. Take from us our need to return blow for blow, hit for hit, no matter how cloaked these actions are within us. Make us humble in your presence. Help us to live in the truth of who we are, beloved ones created in your image yet in need of your constant help. Amen. *Mitakuye Oyasin.*

Retreat Session Three

Driving from Colorado to North Dakota in January, 1997, on icy roads which seemed always to reach the horizon, I recalled that before 1877 these plains were home for Black Elk and the people of the Upper Plains. He must have survived many such winters because the memory of them led him to pray from his heart:

"O Great Spirit of the North, Waziah,[4] *purifier of the earth, purifier of all that is unclean within the soul of the two-legged!"*[5]

Why would he plead in his opening prayer to the directions, not for warmth and cozy comfort, but for spiritual cleansing? Because for a man who grasped that earth was the place of his spiritual endeavor, the hardship of winter was a time of spiritual purification and cleansing of soul. Winter reduced his people to survival level. For Black Elk, it was a time for facing and balancing the dark emotions of inner turmoil—hatred and fear—putting them in their rightful place, in humility before *Wakan-Tanka.* As the freezing temperatures reduce one who is unprotected to immobility and helplessness, Black Elk understood winter as a time for purification of the heart's pride, of hubris, self-importance and the need for revenge.

Black Elk looked to the North not only to purify and cleanse his heart, but also to purify his people before *Wakan-Tanka.* In the girl's puberty ceremony he prays:

"O you, giant Waziah, Power of the [N]orth, who guard[s] the health of the people with your winds, and who purif[ies] the earth by making it white, you are the one who watches that path upon which our people walk. Help us especially today with your purifying influence...!"[6]

His people had true respect for winter; they spent

each summer preparing to face the worst it could deal them. Watching for and surviving many winters had shaped within them a rightful fear for the power coming from the North and they named it *Waziah* (the giant). Only those left at the mercy of bitter cold and wind would personify the season as a giant. In winter, the stiff northern winds rule; Black Elk felt this was the ideal time to acknowledge our human need for divine help and to cleanse overgrown pride.

By cleansing them of excessive pride, the season helped the people to grow in the Lakota virtue of humility. Humility is the proper stance before *Wakan-Tanka*. In the ritual of Sun Dance, Black Elk describes what the dancers must wear to hold themselves in a proper attitude as they dance toward the center to sacrifice themselves:

"...dancers put on soft rabbit fur because it represents softness, gentleness and humility which we must possess if we are to go to the center of the earth."[7]

This interior attitude kept his people walking the straight way of the Red Road. But the, earth too, shares in the need for the balance which humility gives. Black Elk prayed for its cleansing by winter winds and freezing cold in order that the earth, *Unci Maka*, would come to life in spring in a new fresh way.

Thus, whenever he began his ritual prayer for seeking a vision with the *inipi*, he faced North acknowledging the purifying power of God manifested there. The sweatlodge ceremony was fundamental to spiritual purification for the Lakota and no less so for Black Elk. His daughter Lucy relates how even after he retired from his position as catechist he prayed in a "sweat" with his friends.[8] In the last years of his life, he described in detail the meaning of all objects in this ritual in the following way:

The rite of the onikare [another word for sweatlodge]

utilizes all the powers of the universe: earth and the things which grow from the earth, water, fire and air. The water represents the Thunder-beings who come fearfully but bring goodness, for the steam which comes from the rocks, with which is the fire, is frightening, but it purifies us so that we may live as Wakan-Tanka wills, and He may even send to us a vision if we become pure.[9]

As we contemplate the power of God's creation coming from the north, let us enter more deeply in this retreat with Black Elk by praying for cleansing and purification of our hearts, souls and entire life. Facing the North, most of all, means asking for purification of heart and conscience motives, of our soul's overt and hidden egoism.

There are many time-tested ways to seek spiritual purification of all that stands between us and God, *Wakan-Tanka*. One way that Black Elk knew to help his spirit express its cry for vision was fasting from food and drink.

On November 14, 1906, Father Buechel made the following entry in his diary:

> "Nick Black Elk had come to collect money at an issue in Rosebud. As it came off later, he made three days retreat. I gave [it] to him. He asked, 'How is it about eating during the retreat? The Indians do not eat during their recesses.'" The incident here reveals Black Elk's attempt to understand his newer religious practice in the context of his older one. Fasting was common to both traditions.[10]

If it is possible for you to actually participate in a sweatlodge ceremony, it will be helpful to your prayer with Black Elk. But any form of fasting, perhaps for one day, or maybe eating and drinking in moderation throughout the retreat, will be beneficial. The fast is not only for the sake of physical health, but primarily a way to free yourself from a focus on the body, leaving your spirit free to commune with *Wakan-Tanka*, God.

If abstaining or reducing your food intake is difficult or impossible for you, there are other ways to fast. For instance, you might attempt to purify your thoughts of all noise and interior dialogue. You might close out the many sources of information which bathe us with a superfluity of messages: radio, television, the constant presence and sound of cassettes, newspapers, magazines, shopping malls, the Internet and cheap novels. With this chaos of information and sound made silent, we prepare ourselves to enter the spiritual universe of Black Elk. He understood that only in the silence and truth of communion with God does true vision come.

The place to begin seeking this truth is with feet on the earth, fully acknowledging its power and honoring it as God's greatest creation. Make this attitude of Black Elk's your own.

Our prayer for cleansing will help us to face the imbalances which exist in our world today—a world where twenty percent of the earth's population consumes eighty percent of its resources. To begin to find a balance between the needs of our relatives and the earth's resources, we must begin with a balance in our own hearts and bodies.

For Reflection

- *Go to your place of prayer, quiet yourself. In the presence of all your relatives ask yourself what you must do to create a greater balance in the sacred hoop.*

- *Try to remain always in the silence, keeping that same*

sense of calm and perspective in your everyday life that you
develop in prayer. You slowly begin to perceive the one way
to open your entire self for purification.

- Stay away from self-recriminating thoughts and guilt
  about your actions and life-style. These will only impede
  the clarity for which you "cry out." Stand with Black Elk
  on the Good Red Road of blessings. If your mind wanders,
  gently discipline your inner self to cry out to the Great
  Spirit to fill you with gratitude for the original beauty and
  exquisite balance inherent in nature surrounding you in all
  directions.

- Beginning with gratitude for your body—your closest
  relative, which has served you and has carried you thus far
  in life—let your spirit wander slowly where it is led to
  contemplate the circles of blessing which surround you in
  your life.

- True purification of soul is balanced with gratefulness.
  What acts of gratitude will you offer during this retreat?

Closing Prayer

O Father and Grandfather Wakan-Tanka, you are the
source and end of everything. My Father Wakan-Tanka, you are
the One who watches over and sustains all life. O my
Grandmother, you are the earthly source of all existence! And
Mother Earth, the fruits which you bear are the source of life
for the earth peoples. You are always watching over your fruits
as does a mother. May the steps which we take in life upon you
be sacred and not weak!

Help us O Wakan-Tanka to walk the red path with firm
steps. May we who are your people stand in a wakan manner,
pleasing to you! Give us strength which comes from an

understanding of your power! Because you have made your will known to us, we will walk the path of life in holiness, bearing the love and knowledge of you in our hearts! For this and for everything we give thanks![11]

Notes

[1] Brown, p. 12.

[2] Glancy, p. 40.

[3] Brown, p. 40.

[4] *Wazi'ya* is a proper noun: the name for, and personification of power and nature characteristic of North (Eugene Buechel, *A Dictionary—Wowapi Wan of Teton Sioux* [Pine Ridge, S.D.: Red Cloud Indian School, 1983]).

[5] Brown, p. 20.

[6] Brown, p. 119.

[7] Brown, p. 85.

[8] Steltenkamp, p. 60.

[9] Brown, p. 31.

[10] Steltenkamp, p. 60.

[11] Brown, p. 14.

Day Four

The East: "The Morning Star" *Wisdom*

The Sun, the light of the world,
I hear him coming.
I see his face as He comes.
He makes the beings on earth happy,
And they rejoice.
O Wakan-Tanka, I offer to you
this world of light.[1]

You will do well to be attentive to this as to a lamp shining
in a dark place, until the day dawns and the morning star
rises in your hearts.[2]

Coming Together in the Spirit

In the thirty years since my first encounter with Black Elk's books, my understanding of him has grown, as has his reputation among Native Americans and the general public. I now consider myself his devotee and disciple; he is also my brother in Jesus Christ. We share the life that Jesus came to bring as "the morning star" who rises in our hearts and "the Sun, the Light of the world."

It was in the early fifties when *The Sacred Pipe* was published. It contained seven sacred rituals of the Oglala Lakota as described by Black Elk to Joseph E. Brown. I was a stranger to Black Elk then and even a stranger to my own Lakota history and heritage and to myself. This book opened a world of spiritual knowledge to me. It was like a morning star on the dark horizon of my post-reservation existence.

I cannot remember exact words from that first reading but an awareness of the *wakan*, the holy, evoked by his words filled me and remained with me to this day. It was as though I had witnessed a spiritual eclipse of the sun: Though he was still a mystery to me, I had a sense of the sacredness in his words and being. I consider my understanding of his teaching limited, then as now. But that one spiritual glimpse of the *wakan* surrounding him caught me. For me, this was a first step toward profound self-understanding, self-respect and acceptance. We all have moments like this: thin points of light, insignificant at first, yet they become moments of encounter with life's mystery and truth. As you face the East, do you remember such points of light in your life?

Defining Our Thematic Context

In the late 1960's, while teaching at Red Cloud School at Pine Ridge, South Dakota, I visited Black Elk's granddaughter, Olivia, who lived in the village. At my request, she related her childhood memories of her grandfather, most of which were of the last years before he died. She said he was an old man, shrunken by age and suffering; her family looked after his needs. They even carried him from place to place while he prayed the rosary constantly toward the end. When he was stronger, he prayed on the hill with the sacred pipe. Beyond this she could remember little more. Her candidness and willingness to share with me are vivid memories yet today. Though I promised to return for further visits, I did not. But after that I began to make pilgrimages to Black Elk's grave site at St. Agnes Catholic Church in Manderson, where he spent a good portion of his life. At that time, though I was a young Catholic sister, the place for my people in the Catholic Church was not clear to me.

As I understood my people, we seemed disjointed and out of place in the Catholic Church: We were too poor to contribute much to its endeavors; we were still considered missionary material after hundreds of years of evangelization; our promising young men and women were departing from the practice of their Catholic faith; enthusiasm for many Church activities was lacking. These perceptions left me uneasy and I've spent most of those thirty years attempting to understand this uneasiness. In pilgrimages to Black Elk's grave I pleaded with his spirit to help us find a way to live with dignity in this world.

In retrospect, I can understand now that knowledge of him led me to knowledge of Jesus Christ—and of myself. In these years, as I've continued to search and learn, I realize that my entire journey with Black Elk has been a blessing of the East and of the Daybreak Star. Just as his own life moved through gradual shades of understanding, so has mine. Every healthy human life grows and expands beyond itself, just as his did. Let us pray earnestly for all peoples of the earth that every person will live healthily and expand spiritually to serve others. This is the Lakota way.

Opening Prayer

O *Wakan-Tanka Tunkashila*, you alone are the source of all spiritual enlightenment and understanding. Your Son, Jesus, came among us like a light in darkness to allow us the spiritual understanding to change our lives and to walk on the Good Red Road.

O Great Spirit, help *my people* to *understand the greatness of our own tradition.* Use this *book to bring peace on the earth, not only among men but within all human beings and between the whole of creation.* In this retreat we seek your spiritual light. *Help us to understand well that all things are the works of the Great Spirit. Help us to know that the Great Spirit is within all things: the trees, the grasses, the rivers, the mountains, and all the four-legged animals, and the winged peoples…. Help us to understand this deeply in our hearts so that we will fear, love, and know the Great Spirit. Then we will live and act as you intend.* Amen.[3]

Retreat Session Four

After 1881, when Black Elk acted out the Horse Dance portion of his vision, the direction of East became a moving power and source of spiritual understanding for him. Also, the Daybreak Star, given to him in his great vision by the third grandfather, evoked the essence of his sacred calling. These gifts were synonymous with his role as spiritual guide and healer of the people. The image of the dark predawn sky pierced by the brilliant morning star signified wisdom for him throughout his life. In his great vision, the third grandfather addressed him while giving him the third cup:

Pointing the cup of water to me he said: "Behold this; like unto this you shall live." There was a star in the third cup of water. He said again: "On earth the beings will be glad to see you. So take courage. Now you shall go forth back to your mother earth." Through this morning star in the cup of water I was to get all my wisdom to know everything.[4]

Yet, the morning star meant more than his medicine power and ability to conjure it. It symbolized the wisdom of the Good Red Road. The predawn darkness, the morning star and the slow dawning of light embodied the spiritual understanding given him by God, *Wakan-Tanka*. This knowledge was the way to walk the two roads of life, the Red of blessings and the Black of anguish and contradiction.

We can see this in Black Elk's teaching about the seven sacred rites of the Oglala. For example, the Daybreak Star played a significant role in his explanation of the Lakota central rite of the Sun Dance. There the darkness of ignorance can be cured by the Sun Dance ritual, *Winwang Wacipi*. In the following quotation, the sun dancers are told why they dance:

...it is only the ignorant person who sees many where there really is one. This truth of the oneness of all things we understand a little better by participating in this rite, and by offering ourselves as a sacrifice.[5]

In another instruction regarding the central symbols of the Sun Dance, he states:

A five-pointed star should be cut from rawhide. This will be the morning star who stands between darkness and the light and represents knowledge.[6]

For Black Elk, ignorance is a state wherein human beings allow divisions and boundaries to dominate their lives, hemming them in. For him this was true darkness, for it kept them from seeing the world of *Wakan-Tanka* as it really is.

From the time he performed the Horse Dance part of his great vision at Fort Keough[7], he began to rise and pray with the morning star in order that this ignorance be taken from him. His people joined with him as their *wicasa wakan*. Even as an eighteen-year-old he was their bridge with the *wakan* world. They began praying with him and the morning star; together they cried out to know the ways of wisdom:

I usually get up about the time the morning star rises and my people were to have knowledge from this star and people seemed to all know this. They were eager to see it come out and by the time the [D]aybreak [S]tar came out the people would be saying, "Behold the star of wisdom."[8]

Rising early and praying with the morning star taught him a time-honored contemplative truth—wisdom grows out of solitude and silence. It deepened his conviction that he was part of a vast, incomprehensible reality, a relative to all.

In 1904, at forty, he complied with the Catholic Church's process for Lakota converts and renounced the Lakota ways. In 1907, he became a Catholic catechist; seemingly a severe test for his vision. He must have struggled to understand and meld the unseen world of his vision with this work which seemed to contradict what he stood for and who he was. As his life continued, these two worlds became one.

Besides carrying the memory of his vision, Black Elk was responsible for his growing family, as well as for healing among his people. He, who trained to be a master horseman, warrior and hunter, was forced to provide for his family with government-issued food and materials. Perhaps an even greater leap to the "other" was his entrance into the literate *wasicu* world. Here, having a hands-on relationship with the natural environment mattered not; his livelihood depended upon his ability to perform—to work according to the *wasicu* definition. By that definition, literacy was crucial. Black Elk never spoke English but learned to read and write in his dialect, Lakota.

It must have seemed a step removed from the immediacy of his former way of life. Yet, if his great vision was to have any significance for others, it had to carry him into and through this new *wasicu* world without damage to his spiritual integrity. He chose to live out his vision by becoming a Catholic and some would say he became a good—even a great—Catholic.

At the end of his long years as a catechist, he dictated the knowledge given him in his great vision so that it would not be lost. It appears from the witness of his life that Black Elk embraced two religious traditions whole-heartedly; he gave himself to both and lived them fully. Not a contradiction or paradox this, but the blessing of the East in Black Elk's life. At its heart, it was the gifted intuition that *all being is one. Mitakuye Oyasin!*

This may present us with an intellectual puzzle, but for him it was the fruit of his recognition of the relatedness of all things. This insight played itself out in a life of spiritual integrity. So, the meaning of the East lies within his holistic view of himself as "related to all beings" because for him, all being is one. The Catholic and Lakota traditions, at heart, were one; for this unity Jesus prayed on the night before he died.[9]

The sacred direction of East served as one of the most powerful helpers on his journey through life. For him, though there was only one God, *Wakan-Tanka*, in his Lakota tradition, that same One was the Father, Son and Spirit in the Catholic tradition. This was not an intellectual problem for him to solve. His gifted soul rather allowed it to be. He entered into it, as only he could, rather than work to solve it.

Black Elk's was an intuition of highest nature and it followed the intellectual route as far as it could take him. Then it leaped beyond to the level of spiritual under-standing which marked and grounded him. Many of us are called to live this level of spiritual intuition as well; we are simple human beings just as he was.

The knowledge he left to us has made Black Elk a culture bearer of enormous significance. Not just for the Lakota and Native Americans, but for all human beings who will listen. As he did, so we must seek the understanding to find and build a "new culture of love."[10] As we stand at the threshold of a new millennium for our globe and its people, let us face East with Black Elk and send our voices toward the first light on the horizon. Let us cry out, as he did, for spiritual understanding and wisdom to carry it out.

For Reflection

- *Rise early to pray with the morning star. Though it may not be visible to your eyes, it hangs there in our dark hearts.*

- *Go to your center, call the entire cosmos to join your prayer to the East. What serves as the morning star, the herald of spiritual understanding, in your own life?*

- *Reflect upon spiritual understanding in your life. How has it kept you on the Good Red Road? Recall specific events and examples. How has this understanding served you during your walk on the Black Road of contradictions, sorrow and anguish?*

- *Whether we like it or not, we, too, are culture bearers. In this retreat we have reason to question ourselves: What culture shall we bear into the future? Can we find the best in the cultures we see today?*

- *Black Elk's great gift of the East was an intuition that as God is One, all being is one. Can we understand this unity and build a new culture upon it? Can we find the place at which they meet, as Black Elk did?*

Closing Prayer

My relatives all—listen! Wakan-Tanka has been kind to us, and has placed us upon a sacred Earth; upon her we are now sitting…. For the good of you all Wakan-Tanka has taught to me in a vision, a way of worship—this I am now teaching to you. The heavens are sacred, for it is there that our grandfather, the Great Spirit, lives… These heavens are as a cloak for the universe—this robe is now upon me as I stand here. O Wakan-Tanka, I show to you the sacred hoop of our nation, which is this circle within which there is a cross…/ And I show you the earth which you have made, and which you are always making…. The never-ending light which turns the night into day, we also wear, that the light may be amongst our people, that they may see. I show to you also the Morning Star which gives knowledge to us.[11] *Mitakuye Oyasin!* Amen.

Notes

[1] Brown, p. 83.

[2] 2 Peter 1:19.

[3] Adapted from Brown.

[4] DeMallie, pp. 139-140.

[5] Brown, pp. 94-95.

[6] Brown, p. 71.

[7] DeMallie, pp. 215-226.

[8] DeMallie, p. 226.

[9] John 15.

[10] A "new culture of love" is taken from Pope John Paul II's encyclical on evangelization. He offered a challenge to the entire world to work for healing of the spirit of the world and thereby form a new culture. See Avery Dulles, "John Paul II and the New Evangelization," *America*, Feb. 1, 1992, p. 166.

[11] Brown, p. 82.

Day Five

The South: "The Blooming Tree"
Generosity

"By south wind is meant the Holy Spirit who awakens love."— Saint John of the Cross

O You who control the sacred winds, and who live there where we always face, Your breath gives life; and it is from you and to you that our generations must come and go.[1]

Coming Together in the Spirit

To understand the teaching of Black Elk, we need a contemplative outlook. And a reading of mystical literature in the Catholic tradition will show that the heart of all mystical awareness is precisely the oneness of all being. The poem below, written by a Carmelite nun and inspired by Saint John of the Cross, one of the greatest mystics in the Catholic tradition, reveals a mentality much like Black Elk's.

Defining Our Thematic Context

Come, South Wind

Over and over I say to the south wind: come, waken in me and warm me!

I have walked too long with a death's chill in the air,
mourned over trees too long with branches bare.
Ice has a falsity for all its brightness
and so has need of your warm reprimand.
A curse be on the snow that lapsed from whiteness,
and all bleak days that paralyze my land.

I am saying all day to Love who wakens love:
rise in the south and come!
Hurry me into springtime; hustle the winter
out of my sight; make dumb
the north wind's loud impertinence. Then plunge me
into my leafing and my blossoming,
and give me pasture, sweet and sudden pasture.

Where could the Shepherd bring
his flocks to graze? Where could they rest at
    noonday?
O south wind, listen to the woe I sing!
One whom I love is asking for the summer
from me, who still am distances from spring.[2]

—Jessica Powers

The author addresses the South wind as though it can
really understand her. She speaks of many creatures of
the earth as someone who is familiar and well known to
them. She also identifies the movements of her soul
which feels cold and dark, "distances from spring" with
the earth's seasons.

It is important to emphasize the fact that Black Elk
shares insights and intuitions with Francis of Assisi who
also was thrust into profound communion with all living
beings. As we read the poem for today's preparation, we
cry out to be drawn into this contemplative spirit which
sees the oneness of all being.

Opening Prayer

Wakan Tanka Tunkashila, you have given us life to walk on the good red road and face the storms of the Black Road. Today, we thank you for your blessings and goodness to us through the summer winds that warm us and nourish the earth that the tiny faces of grass can show on the earth. Let our lives be as thanksgiving songs to you as we stand with our brother, Nicholas Black Elk, facing the South. Amen.

RETREAT SESSION FIVE

"The South brings the warmth" and "your breath gives life" are two phrases used by Black Elk to speak of and address the South. They also recall one of earth's most precious gifts to us—the breeze, or "the breath of life." Inherent within the breeze is nature's balance: between the merciless winds of deep winter and the scorching, unbearable winds of the desert, the breeze is a perfect blend of both. As the Lakota protected themselves from and were spared the wrath of the North's bitter winds, so they opened themselves to the warm winds of the South. One balanced the other; balance and equilibrium: This is the spiritual focus in the sacred hoop.

The winds from the South are especially *wakan* because they bring the fullness and flowing of life within the sacred hoop. The blooming tree at the center of the soul of the people flourishes because of the South. To know the earth as the Lakota did, handing down centuries of quiet observance of the habits of all living beings through stories and rituals, shows us how to live well among ourselves and with nature.

Black Elk's people had lived unknown generations storing their memories in a way which would help them survive and teach them to learn patterns of relationship with nature. They had learned to scrutinize the slightest movements of the wind—gauge its direction and remember the scents and sounds it carried. As their lives were dominated by the earth's forces, they negotiated respectful, balanced ways to live with these forces.

Stretching from North to South in the image of the sacred hoop is the good red road of blessings. When walking the red road facing South, they walk respectfully on the earth, in balance. Black Elk prayed in the Keeping/ Releasing of a Soul ceremony that through this rite the people would walk the earth firmly with *wakan* steps.

O You, sacred Earth, from whence we have come, You are humble, nourishing all things; we know that you are wakan and that with You we are as relatives. Grandmother and Mother Earth who bear fruit, for You there is a place...[in our lives]. O Mother, may Your people walk the path of life, facing the strong winds! May we walk firmly upon You! May our steps not falter! We and all who move upon You are sending our voices to Wakan Tanka! Help us! All together as one we cry: help us![3]

In another prayer to the South in the ritual *Ishna Ta Awi Cha Lowan*, Making a Woman ceremony, he addresses *Wakan-Tanka* as he faces South, in the following way:

Grandfather, Wakan-Tanka, behold us! You have placed a great power there where we always face, and from this direction many generations have come forth, and have returned. There is a winged One at this direction who guards the sacred red path, from which generations have come forth. The generation which is here today, wishes to cleanse and purify itself that it may live again![4]

As his people have received life itself from the South, so they will return there when they die, as to their source.

Thus, he refers to the South as the place where Lakota generations come and go. His prayers in preparation for sweatlodge ceremony, speak of the South as a direction of great power which "we always face." The Winged One is a white swan who guards the Good Red Road.

One traditional way to respect earth and to live nobly upon her is the tradition of dance. Until the advent of affordable indoor heat, the greatest number of dances were celebrated during the time of the South—spring, summer and early fall. In one of the most sacred Lakota dances this respect is manifested doubly by honoring "winged creatures." The Men's Traditional Dance[5] imitates the prairie chicken, and frequently dancers raise a dance staff in honor of *Wakan Tanka* or circle the staff in the air to honor the directions. Also, the Men's Grass Dance originally was a *wakan* dance which both honored and celebrated the close bond between the Lakota and the earth.

From oral history[6] comes the meaning of the traditional role of Grass dancers. Their dancing was to communicate with and imitate the grass people, who had a right to live also. Grass dancers were to dance over the grass, gently tamping it down, flattening it so that no dancer coming after would hurt a foot on bumpy surface. The Grass Flattening Song, *"Taku Wakan mani. Kokipa pelo,"* means: "Something holy is walking. They fear it." The dancers showed honor to the grass by imitating its movement through limber side-to-side movements. The origin of many dances[7] was to honor nature by expressing the heart's cries through the body to *Wakan Tanka.* Nowhere did Black Elk sense this need to express and celebrate gratitude more than when he stood facing the South.

It is not possible to understand the profound meaning of the South without looking briefly at the rite of Keeping and Releasing of Soul,[8] in which the South plays a crucial role. The rite is a means of facing and dealing with the death of one beloved by family and tribe. It is a year-long ritual which keeps the memory of the deceased alive so that soul of the deceased may live in a greater way. During the year, the soul is ritually cleansed, purified and prepared for the day of its release to journey South, to the place of its source. There it is to join all the spiritual powers of the universe—and all living beings—and live in a new way.[9]

The instructions for this rite are precise and highly symbolic, including the participation of four virgins to enhance the purity of the ritual. During the ritual, the soul dwells in a special tipi constructed for it. It is kept symbolically in a *wakan* bundle (the keeping bundle) along with the deceased's favorite items. The tipi is constructed with its door facing South because, at year's end, this is the direction the soul must journey. The keeping bundle is carefully lodged in the center of the tipi at the "soul post" to indicate the balance of this ceremony. If the community helps to purify the soul with its reverent behavior and actions, at year's end the *wanagi* will be able to make the spirit journey along the Milky Way back to the South.

During the year, the people are instructed to visit the tipi and, while there, act in a *wakan* manner. If they fail to act respectfully, their actions might hinder the purification of the loved one's spirit. Then, being impure, the soul will be unable to cross to the South and will wander the earth restless and troubled until another Releasing of Soul ceremony. Because the soul remains in their midst within the "spirit tipi," the people themselves are holy and must act like it: no fighting, dissension, violent words or actions, especially when they visit the tipi. Finally, on the day of release called "The Making of Sacredness Day," through an elaborate ritual, the soul is released and all the people join in to send it on its way along the "spirit trail," the Milky Way.[10] This is a happy day because now the soul, purified by the goodness of life and ritual, will live at the heart of the people. This will make the people live, too, in the spirit of the symbolic blooming tree at the center.

The gift of Black Elk lies in the intuition that we "always face this direction." That is, we face death even when life is at its fullest and most fruitful. This rite neutralizes the terror of death and promises a life beyond. Demonstrating the power of the South for the Lakota is the tradition of death songs which draw their strength from the bounty of the South. In our later discussion of the West we will see how some have faced death singing a song unique to their lives. The fullness of life for which it is sung—and the life beyond the South with relatives who have gone before, gives meaning to the stark reality of death. Death does not mean doom. It means a change to a fullness of life.

Given this brief explanation of the South's predominant symbolism, we may find it easier to understand why *generosity* continues to be a highly important value among many contemporary Native American tribes. Its meaning returns to a spiritual source: The earth manifests its greatest gifts after the South winds blow in the summer.

Wakan-Tanka created the earth which in turn provided food, clothing, medicines and a firm foundation to the people with manifest, overflowing, unending generosity. The Lakota strove to imitate such bounty and wealth through being generous.[11] The ritual "giveaway," still practiced today by many tribes is a clear, even countercultural, custom of this ancient belief about the nature of *Wakan-Tanka* who created the earth. The giveaway demonstrates the magnanimous nature and great character of the gifter, *Wakan-Tanka*.

Black Elk speaks further of this generosity. After the soul was released there was great rejoicing in the camp:

When this, the rite, is finished and then the people all over the camp are happy and rejoice...Gifts are given out to the poor and unfortunate ones, and everywhere there is feasting and rejoicing. It is indeed a good day.

Hetchetu welo![12]

In his explanation at the end of the *Ishna Ta Awi Cha Lowan*, the Preparing for Womanhood ceremony, a feast is spread out for all the people. Food is prepared so that all who participated in the ritual as well as onlookers may experience the generosity of *Wakan Tanka* provided by the family of the girl. The young woman at the center of the ritual mixes among the people and there is a great outpouring of generosity.

All the people then said "Hi ho! Hi ho!" and everybody was rejoicing and happy because of the great thing which had been done that day. White Buffalo Cow Woman Appears was brought out of the tipi, and all the people rushed up to her and placed their hands upon her, for now she was a woman, and, because of the rites which had been performed for her, there was much holiness in her. There was then a great feast, and a "give away," and those who were poor received much. It was in this manner that the rites for preparing a young girl for womanhood were first begun, and they have been the source of much holiness, not only for our women, but for the whole nation.[13]

In Black Elk's understanding of life's bountiful goodness, the reality of death was an integral part. This realization was celebrated through ritual, dance and the "giveaway" as a means of imitating *Wakan Tanka*'s openhanded goodness and care. In this way the power of South was a symbol of the journey through life towards death.[14] We, who have learned to shun death and pretend it is not there, have much to learn from Black Elk's prayer to the South.

For Reflection

- *Spend time facing south and remembering some of the blessings of your life. What experiences have helped you to live out the "balance" of the good red road?*

- *Remember and relive some of the greatest acts of generosity you have received during your life. Remember times when you were generous to others.*

- *Do you ever feel inclined to dance for joy? What are the occasions for this desire?*

Closing Prayer

Hee-ay-hay-ee-ee! [four times]. *I am sending a voice to You, O Wakan-Tanka—to You who have always been, and who are above all things. Father, Wakan-Tanka,*

You are the chief of all things; everything belongs to You, because it is You who have created the universe. Upon this great Island You have placed our people, and You have given us the wisdom to know all things. You have made us know the moon and the sun, the four winds and the four Powers of the universe. We know that the generations come from, and return to, that place towards which we always face, and upon this straight red path leading to where the giant lives we have walked in a sacred manner. And above all, we know that Wakan-Tanka...gives strength to the generations to come who will inherit the earth; and the steps that they take will be firm, and they will be free from the darkness of ignorance...[that] they will rejoice as they walk hand-in-hand with their children. Help them to walk the sacred path without ignorance. May the heavens above behold us here and be merciful to us! ....Father, Wakan-Tanka! May we always do and know Thy will. May we never lose this relationship established here! May we cherish it and love it always! O Wakan-Tanka, be merciful to me, that my people may live! Amen.[15]

Notes

1. Brown, p. 51. From the sweatlodge ceremony, emphasis added. In Black Elk's hoop image, when one walks the Good Red Road, one faces South.

2. Jessica Powers, *Selected Poetry of Jessica Powers*, eds. Siegfried and Morneau (Kansas City, Mo.: Sheed & Ward, 1989).

3. Brown, p. 20.

4. Brown, p. 41. The Winged One is the white swan who guards the red road at the South, so that souls approaching it may truly pass over.

5. During this dance when elder men are involved, the people are asked to stand during it, to show respect for this time-honored dance.

6. Michelle Eagle Elk, descended from a line of medicine people, related this.

7. Even war dances were a means of communicating with various powers of nature by way of supplication.

8. Brown, Chapter 2.

9. It is not the purpose of this book to determine to what extent this teaching of Black Elk was influenced by his long association with Catholic doctrine, which is built upon the tenet of life after death.

10. Brown, p. 29, no. 13.

11. This behavior is well documented and need not be belabored here.

12. Brown, p. 126. For a nomadic people, there was also a practicality in "giving away" unnecessary items, large and small, in order to lighten the load carried from place to place.

13. Brown, p. 126; see also p. 100.

14. This same spiritual intuition is found in the spiritual exercises of Saint Ignatius of Loyola where he asks the retreatants to reflect upon the moment of his or her death.

15. Brown, pp. 136-137.

DAY SIX

The West: "The Crucifixion"
Courage

...I could hear the Thunder-beings [from the West]
*calling. I could understand the birds whenever they
sang. When a cloud appeared with the birds it seemed
that they would say: "Behold your grandfathers; make
haste."*[1]

Coming Together in the Spirit

When my father, a Hunkpapa Lakota, died, I held his
arm to feel his last heartbeats. His heart rate was slowing
but persistent. Bending over his ear I encouraged him,
saying: "Don't be afraid, Dad, it's better on the other
side." Shortly thereafter, his heart rate slowed and
gradually stopped. My last encounter was shaped by the
communal experience of our Lakota culture. The courage
to face death has always been of great value to the
Lakota. It crystallizes one's entire life in seconds. As a
daughter, I wanted my father to be brave in these last
moments of his existence. Strength to die comes from the
West which teaches us everyday that all life will come to
an end.

Defining Our Thematic Context

Recently, many Native Americans have examined the Boarding/Mission School Era[2] of our history in the United States. One of the most striking stories about this period tells of Indian children of the late nineteenth century (the time of Black Elk's youth) who were forcibly taken from family and home and sent by train to distant boarding schools. As they were taken away, many of them sang their death songs. Unfortunately, this was no mere exaggeration of childhood fear: Some of those children never returned.

In Black Elk's teaching, singing one's own song in the face of death demonstrates the power of the Spirit world, and the power of the South to give meaning to the stark reality of death. There are stories about Indian warriors from the Plains tribes who would sing their death songs before going into battle. It was seen as the ultimate courage for a human being to sing at that moment. Indeed it is.

Opening Prayer

O *Wakan Tanka*, behold all that we do and ask here! O You Power, there where the sun goes down, who controls the waters. You who come so terribly in order to purify the world and its people, we are about to offer our day to you *Wakan Tanka*, and need your help for we shall remember our life on the Black Road of difficulty and anguish. Today we shall look to our own moment of death; today, we shall listen for our death song. We pray that you will make us sacred. We stand and face the West for we know that we pray not just for ourselves but for generations to come. Give us the strength to stand with outstretched arms at the center with Jesus, the Son of Man and God. Give us his heart, his love and vision. We ask this in his name. Amen.

RETREAT SESSION SIX

In the sacred hoop, the Black Road runs from East to West and signifies the road of suffering, difficulty and anguish. In the Lakota understanding, from the moment of birth until the moment of death, we walk the Black Road because we cannot escape life's turmoil. The long-term remedy to a life dominated by suffering is to stand at the center where the red road balances the black. In this state of balance, human beings are not only centered but also *wakan* because finding and remaining at the center is the will of *Wakan Tanka*.

In the ceremony for making relatives—the *Hunkapi*—Black Elk's most sublime teaching about the center emerges.[3] He believed that the *Hunkapi* ritual established a relationship on earth which most closely resembled that which should exist *"between man and Wakan-Tanka. As we love Wakan-Tanka first and before all else so we should love and establish closer relationships with men...."*[4] Then follows a description of an elaborate ritual filled with symbolic actions which embody the bonding with the Ree people who were traditional enemies of the Lakota. The opening prayer of purification for the ritual is with sweet grass and evokes the world of the sacred hoop with its two roads and the center:

O Grandfather, Wakan-Tanka, behold us! Here we shall make relatives and peace; it is your will that this be done. With this sweet grass which is yours, I am now making smoke, which will rise to you. In everything that we do, you are first and this our sacred Mother Earth is second, and next to her are the four quarters. By making this rite we shall carry out thy will upon this earth, and we shall make a peace that will last to the end of time. The smoke from this sweet grass will be upon everything in the universe. It is good![5]

Again, at the end of the *Hunkapi* making of relatives ceremony, after the long celebration of feasting which follows the rite, he states in the final instructions:

I wish to mention here, that through these rites a threefold peace was established. The first peace, which is the most important, is that which comes within the souls of men when they realize their relationship, their oneness, with the universe and all its Powers, then they realize that at the center of the universe dwells Wakan-Tanka, and that center is really everywhere, it is within each of us.[6]

According to his teaching in these two examples, when you stand at the center the dynamism of the sacred hoop reaches its highest point because, there, humans stand in balance with all the sacred directions. Then the powers of the earth and the symbols of all these directions coalesce dynamically within the soul of the person who stands at the Center with a pure heart.

This is the real Peace, and the others are but reflections of this. The second peace is that which is made between two individuals, and the third is that which is made between two nations. But above all you should understand that there can never be peace between nations until there is first known that true peace which, as I have often said, is within the souls of men.[7]

Without doubt, Black Elk's intuition about the meaning of the center is similar to the teaching of all great world religions. Beyond many of these, however, it demands that the holiness or *wakan* of human beings be one with the integrity of the earth. "Being at the center" describes the balance of human beings who are in right relationship with every aspect of their world. It is crucial to understand that only within this view of the universe does Black Elk's teaching about the Black Road of the West have its deepest meaning. As each day ends, so each life will end.

Praying toward the West enables us to face the prospect of that decisive final moment. In the Lakota tradition, facing West is a reminder of death; whenever we do so is an appropriate time to sing our death songs. Death can be faced with courage when it is done with the strength and healing goodness of the sacred hoop.

On the other hand, Black Elk's perception of the West must be experienced as the powerful wind, lightning and thunderbolts of a summer storm. Then you can imagine why the Thunderbird represents the West. The Thunderbird's function is to *"cleanse the world from filth and to fight the monsters who defile the waters."*[8] The Thunderbird symbolizes clarity in the midst of confusion, and decision in the face of uncertainty.

Thunderbird is really Wakan-Tanka as the great giver of revelation. Purifies [sic] *by strokes of lightning and storms of the West. His symbol is a zig-zag red line forked at each end...it acts as the axis of the world with its lightning connecting heaven and earth.*[9]

Another important aspect of the West is paradox. The truth of *Wakan Tanka* that is revealed to us is such that, at times, it can be manifested only through its contrary. It is like the *heyoka*, or clown, who represents the West's power and is bound to act contrary to what is expected.

In a Pine Ridge community dance of the 1960's, I recall one clown clad outlandishly in horizontally striped clothes, with a large, round, white head, big round eyes and very long nose. At first sight, the *heyoka* frightened me and others with his backward, out-of-step dancing.

The clown poked fun at serious participants, mocking their dancing style with exaggerated movements, teasing adults and children on the side, and generally causing a spectacle. But, as the *heyoka*'s harmlessness became evident, people laughed at its antics and children ran away in play. This figure and dance, along with the symbol of the Thunderbird, attempt to express the unpredictable nature of the Great Mysterious One's actions in human life. The symbols of the West are rich: Suffering, contradiction and paradox are the inevitable realities of life on the Black Road.

Black Elk was called to his great vision by the spirits of the West and given his power from the thunder beings of the West. His own life was deeply marked by that direction's meaning of death and contradiction. Within his lifetime he experienced the cultural death of his people, their apparent spiritual death and the unexpected deaths of his first and second wives, two of his sons and two stepdaughters. In his later years, he lost his reputation as a man of integrity because of seeming contradictions in his religious identity.

Even more, the clarity of his old age was marked by apparent contradiction. The dictation of his vision to John Neihardt in 1931—*Black Elk Speaks*—and later in 1933—*When the Tree Flowers*, which dealt with the mythic background of the Lakota world—from an apparently solid convert to Catholicism was certainly a contrary, unexpected action. In 1947, his final legacy, *The Sacred Pipe*—a ritual book for Lakota ceremonies—was a thunderbolt causing consternation and misunderstanding, especially among Catholic leaders of his time.

Indeed, it was contradictory that a convert of such outstanding character as he, who had grown into an outstanding teacher of the Catholic faith, even a mission-ary to other tribes, left his legacy in terms of the "pagan" religion which he had denounced. His action in this case was protested strongly and publicly by his Jesuit mentor, Father Sialm:

With nine years Nic Black Elk [sic] could for a truth not count the horses which he pretended to have seen in the dream. But perhaps it was rather Mr. Neihardt who by all force put things together to suit his own purpose. Black Elk cannot read the book as it stands and cannot object against the forceful contortion of the poet.[10]

Father Sialm blames Neihardt for the final outcome of the book and roundly discounts *Black Elk Speaks* by citing to the contrary, proof of the old man's career in the Catholic Church:

He has done wonderful good work for the truth & the way & the light which is Christ, and His one holy Catholic apostolic Church. We, as missionaries whom Black Elk calls Fathers, are obliged to protest against the injustices done to Black Elk...[11]

For his part, Black Elk attempted to clarify the situation on January 26, 1934, when he had his daughter Lucy write a public statement again, to the contrary.

I shake hands with my white friends. Listen, I speak some true words. A white man made a book and told what I had spoken of olden times, but the new times he left out. So I speak again, a last word. I am now an old man. I called my priest to pray for me and give me holy oil and the Holy Food, the "Yutapi Wakan." Listen my friends. In the last thirty years I am different from what the white man wrote about me. I am a Christian....[12]

In spite of this protest, he never retracted his words to Neihardt and did leave as his legacy detailed instructions on how to celebrate the Lakota ceremonies in *The Sacred Pipe*. By these actions he became a source of enormous paradox in his life and the history of his people.

A letter from the early 1970's by a Jesuit missionary at Manderson, related to me that to his knowledge Black Elk died a figure of rejection. Members from the two traditions mistrusted him and distanced themselves.[13] The Catholic leaders in his life held him in suspicion because of the widely publicized books about his Lakota teachings. Meanwhile, the Lakota Oglala medicine people looked askance at his conversion to the Catholic faith because he renounced his Lakota practice as devil worship. Though he went on to become an outstanding Catholic, well-known in the region of Manderson and beyond, it caused confusion. With our limited view of life and history, it seems that these actions were opposite and contrary to the normal expectation of such a man.

Yet Black Elk's firm adherence to his own spiritual understanding was a gift of God. Courage, the virtue of the West, sustained him and his people as they walked the difficult Black Road. The strength to support such apparently contradictory traditions with clear conscience can only spring from a profound spiritual source. For Black Elk, the Lakota source was the thunder beings of the West. In this same spirit, the Lakota could sing in the face of death. That is the meaning of this apparent paradox: singing gratefully for one's life in the face of life's crucifixion.[14]

Another paradox of Black Elk's life is the Messiah of his Ghost Dance vision. Although he experienced this vision at the height of the Ghost Dance movement of 1890, he related it to Neihardt years later in 1931. By that time, after twenty-five years as a catechist, it is understandable that his vision of the Messiah was Jesus Christ whom he had preached.

In his vision, Jesus Christ stands at the center of the circle with outstretched arms and pierced hands.

Against the tree I saw a man standing with outstretched arms. As we stood close to him these twelve men said: "Behold him!" The man with outstretched arms looked at me and I didn't know whether he was white or an Indian [sic]. *He did not resemble Christ. He looked like an Indian, but I was not sure of it. He had long hair which was hanging down loose. On the left side of his head was an eagle feather. His body was painted red.*[15]

Jesus is envisioned by Black Elk in the highest way a Lakota man could be, with long hair, at the center of the dance circle, with an eagle feather on the left side of his head, painted red—the color of the Good Red Road. Further, his arms and wounded hands are outstretched in a gesture of open and total generosity. Then the crucified Lakota Christ speaks:

This man said to me: "My life is such that all earthly beings that grow belong to me. My Father has said this. You must say this." I stood there gazing at him and tried to recognize him.[16]

The Crucified One who stands at the core of Catholicism also stands luminous at the center of the hoop at the flowering tree. This is critically important in Black Elk's Lakota-Catholic legacy. This figure of Jesus gathers all the rich symbolism, dynamism and meaning of the center of the circle—as well as the Lakota way and the Catholic way—together into one.

We have as proof of this vision the integrity of the life and death of Black Elk himself.[17] This shows us that he had indeed found the inner peace of union with *Wakan-Tanka*. It was that same integrity which helped him to become a man of compassionate deeds to his people and also, in the Lakota way, a *wicasa wakan* whose actions were *ushica* and *ushimala* for his fellow human beings.

From our sources, we know that Nicholas Black Elk lived two traditions integrally. He grasped the holiness of each, and lived it in a *wakan* way as the cultural boundaries of his time would permit. The power to live such a life can only come from one spiritual source where, within him, the two traditions became one. Out of apparent contradiction flowed a spirit of compassion for all his relatives and his witness to Jesus Christ, an unexpected outcome of Black Elk's *heyoka* calling.

For Reflection

- *Consider the powerful meaning of the West as it culminates Black Elk's life.*

- *Consider the meaning of truth and human understanding of it as it is revealed in history. Where is the real contradiction? Is it not in our limited ability to grasp truth which far exceeds us?*

- *Remember incidents of apparent contradiction in your own experience and life. Do you see their final outcome yet?*

- *Can you recall a moment of clear understanding and light in your own life? A moment of clarity which came like a "flash of lightning showing the way," when, even if only for a brief second, you knew what you should do?*

- *Imagine that you stand facing the West, the final moments of your life. Begin to listen for your own death song, try singing it, write it down so you will remember it after your retreat.*

Closing Prayer

This is a Thanksgiving prayer that Black Elk taught his daughter, Lucy. She recalls, "When our family would get together on Thanksgiving Day, my father would say this prayer. I remember it:

I am talking to you, Grandfather, Great Spirit on this day.
Pitifully, I sit here.
I am speaking for my relatives, my children,
my grandchildren, and all my
relatives—wherever they might be.
Hear me, Grandfather, Great Spirit.

With your help, our needs are taken care of.
You have helped us in the time of want during the past.
And on this day of thanksgiving.
The nations of living things in the world
over—we the two-leggeds, along with the
children and the smaller ones with them—come
to you today to express thanks.

In the future, make us see again a red day of good.
In the past you have preserved us from evil
on this red road.
Keep us on this road and do not let us see anything wrong.

In that future, we shall be without any sin
at all.
And so it will be in the same manner for my
grandchildren and relatives who will follow as well.

We give you thanks, Grandfather
Great Spirit
I am sending this prayer to you." Amen, Amen.[18]

Notes

[1] DeMallie, p. 213.

[2] See Reyhner, John, and Jeanne Eder, *A History of Indian Education* (Billings, Mont.: Council for Indian Education, 1989). The Boarding School Era saw the deliberate fracturing of Indian families by the removal of children to large institutions for white

education.

[3] Brown, pp. 101-115.

[4] Brown, p. 101.

[5] Brown, p. 105.

[6] Brown, p. 115.

[7] Brown, p. 115.

[8] Brown, p. 39.

[9] Brown, p. 39.

[10] Steltenkamp, p. 81.

[11] Steltenkamp, p. 81.

[12] Steltenkamp, p. 83.

[13] Joseph Sheehan, S.J., Pastor at Manderson, South Dakota, in the 1970's by letter responding to my questions regarding the last days of Nicholas Black Elk.

[14] From the Catholic tradition, the only incident of a person singing a death song in my awareness is that of Francis of Assisi who, after he requested that his body be laid upon Mother Earth, sang Psalm 147 to welcome his "Sister Death."

[15] Neihardt, p. 249.

[16] Neihardt, p. 249.

[17] Read further from sources listed in Deepening Your Acquaintance in order to see the strength of Black Elk's integrity as a human being.

[18] Steltenkamp, p. 118, amended.

Day Seven

From the Center
Culture Bearers

"...And I sang in my chains like the sea."
—Dylan Thomas, *"Fern Hill"*[1]

*I...entered the holy place, I walked continually in each
of the four directions, always returning to the center as
you had instructed me.*[2]

Coming Together in the Spirit

As a Lakota woman, I have learned a type of
accommodating silence. This tactic has taught me to
express the truth of what I see from the perspective of my
people in oblique, unoffensive ways. The dynamics of
oppression can either distort human reactions into a bitter
life filled with the static of unforgiveness, or shape a
human being in other ways, as they did with Black Elk.[3]

By his life and demeanor, Nicholas Black Elk has
taught me to embrace the truth of my people; no matter
how heartbreaking it is. Its historic events are only the
outline of the astounding result of deliberate attempts of
one government to obfuscate and recreate the character of
another race. In the face of this reality which he
experienced more deeply than I ever will, he lived a sane
life that was appropriate to both his cultural worlds. He
carried himself with dignity through the most devastating

period of his people.

His life shows me a person with constant awareness of the *wakan* wholeness of the world, even when his world was lying broken around him. If there was truth to be found in his abrupt cultural displacement, it was in Jesus Christ and the strength of the powerful vision of his childhood. He found both and drew strength from them. For me, this gives more credence to his life than anything he dictated. To do this in intelligible, compassionate ways as he did, has been and continues to be, a life task for me.

Defining Our Thematic Context

Through reflection and silence, we have together entered the bicultural world of Black Elk. And at the same time we have allowed the light of his life, as a follower of Christ, to shine upon our own life, making way for our own truth.

By listening to his prayer and even accompanying him in his Prayer of Directions, we have learned a simple method which belies the breadth and depth of its vision and its power. Perhaps it has helped us to situate our own place in our own world which, in truth, is never totally secure. At this point in history, the prophetic traditions of Western culture call us to change our souls' direction from that of consumerism and forgetfulness of the earth. Indeed, praying with Nicholas Black Elk is an exercise of spiritual re-visioning, a profound human and historical conversion.

Opening Prayer

Wakan Tanka Tunkashila, we stand here before you at the brink of a whole new age of our human history. Tunkashila, people of our times have created a great human power, a world of instant global communication. Have mercy on us for we are weak human beings who easily strive for self-interest and personal gain. Help us, Great Spirit, so that the predominant human spirit will not be self-seeking or motivated by greed. Give us wisdom, generosity, courage and the humility to take steps into this new age with pure hearts and clear minds. As we look to the end of this retreat, we ask for strength to remain at the center where the Good Red Road crosses with the black road. Great Spirit, give us enlightenment and a sense of balance on the earth today in all that we think, do, say and pray. For all my relatives! *Mitakuye Oyasin!* Amen.

RETREAT SESSION SEVEN

Nicholas Black Elk is a culture bearer. This means that he embodied and enacted values which have led to spiritual transformation and cultural change.[4] In spiritual terms, culture bearers are described as *"...individuals who...are deeply transparent to the Holy Spirit [Wakan-Tanka] and give voice to ideas that express the loving will of the Spirit for humankind as a whole."*

These ideas, in turn, serve as symbols, drawing the minds of others toward their common source in the ground of consciousness, for some [sic] effecting a spiritual transformation that reflects the changes needed throughout that culture.... The essential attribute of such individuals is that...of surrender.

By surrendering ever more thoroughly to the Spirit within, the individual may become a more concrete expression of change being worked in the culture by the Spirit.[5]

His spiritual life definitely moved in two directions: the way of the earth and the way of late-nineteenth-century Christianity. In the end, the integrity of his life teaches us more about his humanity and about our own potential for integrity. It compels us to listen and reflect because—despite being pulled in two ways—he lived from the profound *wakan* level of his being: his *center*.

In addition to this dichotomy of duality and integrity in his spiritual life, Black Elk wove his life with rich strands of heritage, history, experience and deep reflection.

The first of these strands was the Oglala Lakota. In this area of his life, crucial events were: his birth in 1863; the acting out of his horse vision in 1870; the gradual demise of his people, beginning with Custer's annihilation in 1875; the great cultural divestiture of all Indians in Dakota territory in 1877; his first foray into the *wasicu* world in 1888, and Wounded Knee. This was a fractured world, yet one of vision, of building the deep spiritual foundations that would characterize his life. During this time, he became a prayer leader and healer among his people.

The second strand of Black Elk's life might be one with which many can identify. In it the historical movements of his life were violent and momentous, that is, without warning or a chance for preparation. A crucial bridge event occurred in 1890 during the Ghost Dance movement: Black Elk's vision of Messiah as the crucified Christ standing at the center of the dance circle at the flowering tree. This vision was a seed of what was to come in Black Elk's life.

Though he had been baptized into the Episcopalian

denomination while on tour in Europe, Black Elk's day of baptism into the Catholic church was December 6, 1904. One of the seemingly mundane events which the passage of time has revealed as a powerful event was his entrance into the Native Catechist movement in 1907. During those years he learned[6] the Catholic dogmatic tradition in the Lakota language. We should not underestimate those twenty-plus years he spent immersed in the Catholic catechism, for these years did have an effect upon him. How many times did he retreat to the center crying out for understanding?

The last period of his life, from roughly 1930 to his death on August 17, 1950, saw the recording and publication of *Black Elk Speaks, When the Tree Flowered* and *The Sacred Pipe*. It was a period of intense theological reflection for him. As his daughter and two granddaughters and fellow catechists attest: Black Elk was a thoughtful, intense man who took Catholic teaching seriously, learning it well and passing it on to the best of his ability. He memorized texts from the Scriptures and preached them; he frequently engaged the Lakota-speaking Jesuit priests in long conversations about the symbolism of Catholic and Lakota ceremonies.

Nowadays, we call this type of discussion inter-culturation, inculturation or enculturation.[7] Nearly a hundred years later, we have the language and notions to describe what happens when two diverse cultures meet and interact. Black Elk did not have the words to name his experiences, but neither did anyone in that period. The Jesuit priests with whom he worked were shaped by theological formulations of an earlier era. The word *inculturation* would have sounded strange to them indeed; but this lack of a means of expression does not deny the reality of the experience.

We need to ask why Black Elk found a home in the

Catholic Church. Where did his Lakota world blend with the Catholic world? We must answer this for ourselves while understanding that others say his conversion did not happen or was highly suspect.[8] Without escaping the fact that government policy walked arm-in-arm with aspects of Catholic Indian missions—with undeniable elements of cultural coercion—we cannot deny his wholehearted acceptance of the Catholic faith.

The facts are inarguable that he lived and worked in the Catholic Church for forty years; and he died in his home, a fervent Catholic, blessed with the sacraments. Viewing the reality of his life through nearly a century of constant social change, we risk slighting Black Elk's integrity to say otherwise. By saying he might never have been a Catholic, we second-guess his motives. We assume that from our vantage point, his conversion was coerced, not free.

Yet the clarity of his life at the end speaks of a profound integrity and spiritual healing. There was no language available at that time to express the points of mutuality between the Lakota and the Catholic religions. Nor was religious Catholic society even remotely capable of perceiving either the health of the Lakota ways or the holiness of "Old Nick Black Elk." Yet, for his part, Black Elk looked and found the healthy core of Christianity: Jesus Christ.

What, then, are the places of overlap—places where Black Elk felt some of the old ways were valid? As we end our retreat, we reflect upon the truth of these points so we might return to them as an eternal source and center:

- The tradition of *wakan* as carried out in ritual. The rituals were heavy with the symbolic meaning of sacred persons, objects, clothing, food, language, actions. The Roman Catholic Church at his time and even yet today has an extensive history of sacred ritual—liturgy.

- A sense of the people—*tioshpaye*, the extended family within Lakota culture—can be seen in Christianity as people caring for one another as described in Lakota *ushikiciyapi*, "they have mercy on one another."

- In the tradition of *inipi*, or the sweatlodge, we find a point of common ground for both Lakota and Catholic, in the need for purification or cleansing to be worthy in God's presence. Although the historic means for spiritual cleansing of the two traditions are different—the sweatbath versus the Sacrament of Reconciliation, or Confession—at their best, they both point to the incomprehensible, great mysterious presence of God, or *Wakan-Tanka*, in human life and how we stand before it.

- Sacred Food, *Yutapi Wakan*, or the Holy Eucharist, became the central focus for Black Elk's Catholicity. Even after his retirement, at a priest's request he would gather the people at a certain location, usually one of the Indian homes, to celebrate the Holy Eucharist, the Mass. Sharing a larger meal in common was and continues to be a central social activity for the Lakota people. In the Mass it was the *Yutapi Wakan*, the spiritual food which is the sacrament of Christ's body and blood.

We should pray with Black Elk as a discipline and as an act of inculturation at the deepest level of the sacred center where the best of two holy traditions unite. His prayer of directions provides a pathway which is fundamentally Catholic because in its symbolism it reaches far beyond itself without demeaning the individual or the world.

If Black Elk, a follower of Christ, left us an example, it is of understanding two traditions and rejecting neither. In his life, he brought unity to them in himself. Black Elk lived these two ancient traditions, though neither his times nor his people were ready for their full integration. In those early silent years of American Indian reservations, the encounter between Western culture and Native culture was like the meeting of an "irresistible force and an unmovable object" which took place in the hidden places of his heart, his center. It is only now that we see the result of Black Elk's long, inner struggle: a clear-headed acceptance of each in the only way possible in his time. When asked why he converted to Christianity, he responded, "My children must live in this world."

The prayer of Black Elk is a pathway for us because it reminds us of the steady place we have beneath us, the earth. In the seemingly bipolar moments of our own struggle with the pain of misunderstanding, confusion and disorientation we can, like Black Elk, find our center on the earth. From there, like him, we cry out for understanding, then absorb the truth of the struggle into our hearts and lives for the sake of "all our relatives" or *Mitakuye Oyasin*. He lived out the truth of himself and in doing this he became a culture bearer. So must we learn like the poet Dylan Thomas and like Nicholas Black Elk who "sang in his chains like the sea."

For Reflection

- *Review each day of your retreat. Recall what understanding you gained in your prayer toward each direction. Create your own prayer of the directions for your life, with room to expand and grow.*

- *Review your own life. When do your feet touch the earth? When are you able to find your center?*

- *What culture are you bearing to the next generation? What culture would you want to offer?*

- *Spend time before the end of your retreat at the center of the circle with Black Elk, with Jesus Christ at the Tree. Speak to Christ at that center.*

Closing Prayer

Wakan-Tanka Tunkashila, Father, Mother of my being! Open my heart, my spirit and soul to hear the words which Black Elk sings:

> *Friend do this! Friend do this! Friend do this!*
> *If you do this, your Grandfather will see you.*
> *When you stand within the holy circle,*
> *Think of me when you send your sacred prayer.*
> *If you do this He will give you all that you ask for.*
>
> *Friend do this! Friend do this! Friend do this!*
> *That your Grandfather Wakan-Tanka may see you.*
> *When you stand within the sacred hoop,*
> *Raise your hand to Wakan-Tanka.*
> *Do this and He will bestow upon you all that you desire.*[9]

Wakan-Tanka Tunkashila, source of our being, thank you for giving us this song through the White Buffalo Calf Woman. Let us sing this song that it may make our hearts good and then we will stand with our brother and friend, Jesus Christ and his disciple Nicholas Black Elk! It is indeed so. *Hetchetu welo!* Amen.

Notes

1 Dylan Thomas, "Fern Hill," *The Collected Poems of Dylan Thomas 1934-1952* (New York, N.Y.: New Directions Publishing Corp., 1971), p. 180.

2 Brown, p. 62.

3 At this moment in history it is imperative to revise our images of the past. We must shake out the dust of ignorance, indifference and forgetfulness accumulated in and around our understanding of American history. Abstract understanding will never be enough; we must revise the images of our Native American history from aggressor to adventurer, from over-controlling parent to companion. This stance presents a truth of our humanity as our source of action. So it is with Black Elk's prayer we join them, make them part of us—in order to move ahead into the future with a wider view. Until we do this we are fooling ourselves.

4 Judson B. Trapnell, "Bede Griffiths as a Culture Bearer: An Exploration of the Relationship Between Spiritual Transformation and Cultural Change." *The American Benedictine Review* 47:3, September, 1996, pp. 260-283.

5 Trapnell, p. 283.

6 Lucy Looks Twice and others of his contemporaries attest to this. See Steltenkamp, Chapters 4 and 5. Recently, in an encounter with his granddaughters Esther Black Elk Deters and Olivia Black Elk Pourier, this observation was confirmed

7 Aylward Shorter, *Toward a Theology of Inculturation* (Maryknoll, N.Y.: Orbis Books, 1989). See Chapter 1 on terminology.

8 See Holler, Chapter 1, also Julian Rice, *Black Elk's Story: Distinguishing Its Lakota Purpose* (Albuquerque, N.M.: University of New Mexico Press, 1994). Rice attempts to disentangle the traditional Black Elk "cleanly" from Western influences on his publications.

9 Brown, p. 131.

Going Forth to Live the Theme

One hundred years ago, Black Elk faced many hard choices: how to express himself within a changed society; how to unify in himself diverse religious traditions; how to survive economically in a world that no longer valued his cultural gifts. We, who live at the dawn of a new century, face similar decisions about how to achieve our spiritual goals in a world threatened by environmental destruction, warfare and rampant materialism. This includes the abstract world of on-line and programmed virtual reality.

The Lakota world of Black Elk counted for nothing in the nineteenth-century schemes of the United States government. He and his people were denigrated as savages, heathens and devil worshipers. The *wasicu* represented a world diametrically opposed to the tradition in which Black Elk had been raised. They had no concept of *Mitakuye Oyasin*, no deep-rooted sense of communion with the earth and all living things. Although they did not know it at the time, they had much to learn from the Lakota holy man whose teachings are even more relevant to us today.

When Joseph Epes Brown first met Black Elk, the anthropologist was struck by Black Elk's innate power, kindliness and strong sense of mission. The holy man shared his wisdom in the hope that those who heard him would be brought back to "the Good Red Road" of spiritual understanding.

How can we who have shared this retreat with Black Elk attain that goal for ourselves and others? By placing ourselves in the center of the sacred hoop of life wherein we recognize our relationship with all living things. By practicing the Lakota virtues of humility, wisdom, generosity and courage in all our relationships with created beings and with *Unci Maka*, Grandmother Earth. By remaining faithful to "the man with outstretched arms" who appeared in Black Elk's Messiah vision and who makes his presence known to each of us who are called by his name. And by seeking that inner and outer unity for which Jesus prayed at the Last Supper, "that they all may be one" (John 17:21).

Deepening Your Acquaintance

The following resources are intended to help you sustain your relationship with Black Elk and to deepen your understanding of Native American cultures.

Books

Brown, Joseph Epes, ed. and recorder. *The Sacred Pipe: Black Elk's Account of the Seven Rites of the Oglala Sioux*, Civilization of the American Indian Series, Vol. 36. (Norman, Okla.: University of Oklahoma Press, 1989, first published 1953). Three years before his death, Black Elk spent several months with Joseph E. Brown relating his understanding of the Oglala ceremonies.

DeMallie, Raymond J., ed. and intro., *The Sixth Grandfather: Black Elk's Teachings Given to John G. Neihardt* (Lincoln, Neb.: University of Nebraska Press, Bison paperback, 1985, first published 1984). From the original stenographic notes of *Black Elk Speaks* and *When the Tree Flowers*.

Neihardt, Hilda. *Black Elk & Flaming Rainbow: Personal Memories of the Lakota Holy Man and John Neihardt* (Lincoln, Neb.: University of Nebraska Press, 1995). Daughter of John Neihardt who witnessed the interviews between Nicholas Black Elk and John Neihardt.

Steltenkamp, Michael F. *Black Elk: Holy Man of the Oglala*, (Norman, Okla.: University of Oklahoma Press, 1993). Lucy Black Elk, daughter of Black Elk, relates her memories of her father as a Catholic catechist.

Videos

"Ancient America: Indians of the West." From The Video Catalogue, 1-800-733-2232.

"Circle of the Spirit: A Saga of Native Americans in the Catholic Church." From the United States Catholic Conference, Washington, D.C.

"Momaday: Voice of the West." From PBS Home Video. 1-800-645-4727.

"The Native Americans." Wellspring Media. 1-800-538-5856.

"Thieves of Time." From PBS Home Video. 1-800-645-4727.

Icons

Available from Bridge Building Images, Inc., P.O. Box 1048, Burlington, VT 05402 (1-802-864-8346) are the following Native American icons in plaques, cards and posters: "Black Elk," "Apache Christ," "Kateri Tekakwitha" and "Navaho Madonna" by Robert Lentz; "Lakota Virgin Mother," "Resurrection," "Lakota Victory Christ" and "Lakota Annunciation" by Father John Giuliani.